D&A e BI

The evolution of data management

Fabrizio Zuccari

"Senza big data analytics, le aziende sono cieche e sorde, vagando sul web come cervi in autostrada."
(Geoffrey Moore)

"Tortura i dati, e confesserano qualsiasi cosa."
(Ronald Coase)

"Without big data analytics, companies are blind and deaf, wandering out onto the web like deer on a freeway."
(Geoffrey Moore)

"Torture the data, and it will confess to anything."
(Ronald Coase)

Table of Contents

Introduction

In an era where the business world is constantly evolving, the ability to understand and make the most of data has become a crucial element for the success of companies.

We live in a digital age, an era in which the amount of data generated every day is extraordinary.
Whether it's business transactions, online customer interactions, or market trends, data has become the new oil.
That's where concepts like Data & Analytics and Business Intelligence come in.

BI and D&A: what are they?

Every single customer interaction, every business transaction, every change in the market contributes to an ocean of information, a vast treasure trove of data that is constantly growing.

In this context of abundance, a critical need arises: to give meaning to this data, to translate it into useful insights that can shape our future path.

This is where two fundamental pillars come into play: *Data & Analytics* (D&A) and *Business Intelligence* (BI).

Data & Analytics:

Data & Analytics represents a set of technologies and processes that allow data to be collected, processed and analyzed.

The main goal is to identify patterns and trends that can offer valuable insights into business performance.

Among the different activities, data analysis allows you to:

- **Constantly monitor business performance:**
  In this context, data analysis is essential in detecting problems early on or identifying areas where operational efficiency can be improved. It acts as a lens that identifies the nuances of business operations in more detail, allowing for quick and

effective intervention where corrections are needed.

- **Identify opportunities for improvement:**
These can range from reducing costs to increasing sales to tangibly improving customer satisfaction. Data analysis acts as a catalyst that reveals potential scope for optimization, allowing companies to develop targeted and pragmatic strategies to achieve precise goals.

- **Predicting future developments:**
Data analytics provides the predictive ability to anticipate crucial trends, such as those in sales, market demand, price dynamics, and competition. This predictive perspective translates into a strategic advantage, allowing companies to take preventive measures or seize emerging opportunities before they fully manifest themselves.

Business Intelligence:

Business Intelligence is a set of tools and techniques that transform data into useful information for decisions. Its applications play a fundamental role in the formulation of strategies and in the definition of long-term business paths:

- **Analysis tool:**
  Through the analysis of trends, customer needs and the positioning of the competition, this discipline offers a clear overview. The ability to understand the market in depth not only provides a detailed picture of industry dynamics, but also allows companies to adapt their strategies in an agile way, anticipating changes and capitalizing on emerging opportunities.

- **Targeted identification of target customers:**
  Through an accurate analysis of customer needs, interests and behaviors, BI offers a penetrating look into the soul of the market. This in-depth understanding of consumer characteristics allows businesses to outline detailed profiles of ideal customers, thereby optimizing marketing strategies and improving the effectiveness of promotional campaigns.

- **Development of new products and services:**
  Based on the analysis of customer needs, BI offers a valuable guide for innovation. This customer-centric approach ensures that new products are optimally aligned with market expectations and demands,

ensuring a timely response to changing industry dynamics.

BI and D&A: what are they for?

The integration between Business Intelligence and Data & Analytics is not only an element of support for business operations, but represents a real enabler for long-term growth and success. Organizations that can harness the full potential of these technologies are able to make more informed decisions, continuously improve their performance, and maintain a competitive edge in an increasingly dynamic and complex global marketplace. Let's see in more detail:

- **Improved Decision Quality:**
  The robust integration between D&A and BI facilitates evidence-based decision-making and rigorous analysis. In an increasingly complex and competitive business environment, decisions made on an intuitive basis or subjective perceptions are no longer enough. The robustness of BI and D&A platforms lies in their ability to aggregate and analyze data from heterogeneous sources, thus providing a complete and accurate picture of the

business reality. This approach allows decision-makers to make informed strategic choices, reducing the margin of error and increasing the likelihood of success. Evidence-based decisions not only improve the effectiveness of the actions taken, but also contribute to greater transparency and accountability within the organization.

- **Business Performance Optimization:**
  By accurately identifying opportunities for optimization and areas for improvement, businesses can monitor and analyze their performance in real-time, identifying areas where action can be taken to improve. Through data analysis, businesses can identify operational inefficiencies, better understand market dynamics, and identify new growth opportunities.
  This analytical process leads to the implementation of targeted strategies, capable of increasing revenues, reducing operating costs and improving customer satisfaction. In practice, BI and D&A provide companies with a holistic view of their operations, enabling a continuous cycle of performance optimization that results in an overall

improvement in market competitiveness.

- **Competitive Advantage and Innovation:**
  In today's rapidly changing and uncertain landscape, the ability to anticipate emerging trends and adapt quickly to new market dynamics is an essential competitive advantage. BI and D&A solutions enable companies to gain a deep understanding of customer behaviors, industry trends, and macroeconomic conditions. This advanced knowledge enables companies to make proactive decisions, develop new products and services in line with market needs, and react promptly to changes in external conditions. In addition, the ability to analyze large volumes of data in real time allows companies to seize opportunities before their competitors, consolidating their presence in the market and maintaining a leadership position.

Basic Definitions

To fully understand the transformative potential of Data & Analytics and Business Intelligence in the business environment, it is essential to further investigate the fundamental definitions of these concepts.

Exploring and interpreting

Exploring and interpreting data within the context of D&A is not simply a matter of technical analysis, but an integrated and strategic process that allows companies to better understand themselves, their market and the opportunities that arise. Only through careful and conscious management of each phase, from collection to interpretation, can data be transformed into a real strategic asset for the organization.

Let's delve further:

Data Collection:

Data collection forms the foundation of the entire analytical process. This phase is essential because it establishes the quality of the raw material on which the subsequent analysis will be based. Data is pulled from a variety of sources, both internal and external, depending on the specific needs of the business. Internal sources include critical systems such as **E**nterprise **R**esource **P**lanning (**ERP**), which manages operational processes and company resources, **C**ustomer **R**elationship **M**anagement (**CRM**), which provides a comprehensive view of customer interactions, and **M**anufacturing **E**xecution **S**ystems (**MES**), which monitors production and operational efficiency. On the other hand, external sources can range from data from social media and websites, which offer insights into consumer behavior and market trends, to data collected from **I**nternet **o**f **T**hings (**IoT**) sensors, which are used to monitor environmental conditions, logistics, and other vital parameters. The quality and completeness of the initial data depend on the correct execution of this phase, which must ensure the collection of accurate, relevant and timely data.

Data processing:

Once the raw data is collected, it needs careful processing to be transformed into useful information. This processing phase includes a series of technical operations aimed at purifying and standardizing the data, making it ready for analysis:

- **Cleaning**:

  It involves removing missing, duplicate, or incorrect data that could compromise the accuracy of the analyses.

  A clean dataset is essential to ensure that the conclusions drawn are based on reliable and consistent data.

- **Transformation**:

  During this step, the data is converted into standardized formats, thus facilitating its manipulation and analysis.

  E.g.: *qualitative variables can be transformed into numerical ones to allow the application of advanced statistical techniques, while different units of measurement are unified to avoid discrepancies in the results.*

- **Normalization**:

    Normalization allows you to standardize data values, making it easier to compare different datasets. This is especially important when the data comes from heterogeneous sources and needs to be combined into a single analysis.

The goal of these operations is to ensure that the data is consistent, reliable, and ready for the next stages of analysis.

- **Interpretation:**

Data interpretation represents the culmination of the D&A process, in which processed data is analyzed to extract meaningful insights that can guide business decisions.

This phase is characterized by the application of advanced techniques that allow you to go beyond the surface of the data to discover its hidden meaning:

- **Statistical analysis**:

    Use mathematical models to identify patterns, trends, and relationships in your data. This type of analysis is critical for understanding data distribution and making inferences about larger populations from limited samples.

- **Machine learning**:

  Machine learning allows you to build predictive models based on historical data, capable of predicting future outcomes or classifying new data based on predefined models. Machine learning applications are particularly useful in contexts such as demand forecasting, supply chain optimization, and customer segmentation.

- **Artificial intelligence**:

  AI goes beyond machine learning, using advanced models to identify complex patterns and insights that even the most experienced analysts may miss. AI is employed in applications ranging from predictive analytics to marketing personalization to real-time business operations optimization.

The ultimate goal of data interpretation is to transform raw data into actionable knowledge that can improve the organization's efficiency, productivity, and competitiveness. Insights gained from accurate data analysis enable businesses to make informed decisions and take strategic actions that can positively influence their future.

Translating and Using

Business Intelligence represents the natural evolution of the practical application of Data & Analytics, acting as a bridge between data analysis and business decisions. Through BI, the results obtained from data analysis are translated into actionable insights, which guide business strategies and facilitate more effective management.

This process is not limited to mere data visualization, but extends to detailed reporting and decision-making intelligence, contributing significantly to the organization's competitiveness.

Let's explore further:

- **Visualization:**

  Data visualization is one of the central elements of Business Intelligence, as it allows you to make the information deriving from data analysis understandable and accessible. In a complex business environment, where decisions must be made quickly, the ability to synthesize large amounts of data into intuitive visual forms is crucial. Data visualization is divided into various tools, each with specific applications:

- **Graphs and charts**:
  These visual tools are critical to clearly representing the relationships, trends, and distributions present in the data. For example, a pie chart is ideal for displaying the percentage composition of various elements, such as the distribution of sales by product, while a bar chart can highlight comparative performance across different regions or time periods. The choice of chart type depends on the nature of the data and the message you want to communicate. Using charts and graphs correctly allows you to quickly identify strengths, weaknesses, and opportunities for improvement.

- **Interactive dashboards**:
  Dashboards are an advanced BI tool, providing an overview of key business metrics through interactive dashboards. These tools aggregate different data visualizations into a single access point, facilitating real-time monitoring of Key Performance Indicators (KPIs). Dashboards not only provide an at-a-

glance overview of business performance, but also allow you to explore data dynamically, giving you the ability to filter, drill down, and compare different dimensions of your business. This interactivity is essential for executives and teams, so they can react quickly to changes in market or operating conditions.

- **Reporting:**

  In addition to visualization, BI extends to reporting, which is a more detailed and structured form of data presentation. Reports provide in-depth analysis on various aspects of the business and are critical tools for decision support.

  Some examples include:

  - **Sales Report**:

    These reports analyze sales performance from multiple perspectives, such as identifying seaonal trends, analyzing the best performing products, and identifying areas that need improvement. Through detailed analysis, you can better understand customer behavior, optimize your product offering, and plan more effective sales strategies.

- **Production Report**:

  Production reporting monitors operational efficiency, production line performance and product quality. These reports are essential for identifying bottlenecks, waste, or defects in production, allowing targeted corrective actions to be taken. In addition, they provide a basis for the continuous optimization of production processes, helping to reduce costs and improve the quality of the final product.

- **Customer satisfaction reports**:

  Evaluating customer feedback through detailed satisfaction reports is crucial to maintaining high levels of service quality and improving the overall customer experience. These reports analyze metrics such as Net Promoter Score (NPS), customer loyalty, and complaint rate, giving you a comprehensive view of the relationship between your business and its customers. The information obtained allows you to identify critical areas and develop strategies to improve customer satisfaction.

- **Decision Intelligence:**

  The real strength of Business Intelligence lies in its ability to support decision-making intelligence, i.e. the ability to interpret and apply data in a way that positively influences business strategic choices. BI tools offer advanced capabilities that assist decision-makers in navigating through complex scenarios:

  - **Trend analysis:**

    Trend analysis allows you to identify patterns over time, such as the seasonality of sales or gradual changes in customer preferences. Understanding these dynamics is essential for planning long-term strategies and anticipating market needs. Early identification of emerging trends can also provide a competitive advantage, allowing the company to be proactive rather than reactive.

  - **Comparative analysis:**

    This technique allows you to compare performance between different business units, time periods, or compared to competitors. Benchmarking is a powerful tool for identifying best practices, recognizing areas that need improvement, and evaluating the effectiveness of different strategies. Decisions based on these comparisons are more informed and allow resources to be allocated more efficiently.

- **Simulations and *What-If scenarios*:** Simulations are predictive tools that allow you to assess the potential impact of different decisions before they are implemented. Through "what-if" scenarios, executives can explore different strategies and choose the most beneficial one based on the simulated outcomes. This ability to anticipate the consequences of decisions reduces risk and increases the likelihood of success.

A synergistic integration

A rigid distinction between Data & Analytics (D&A) and Business Intelligence (BI) is proving increasingly inadequate to address the complex challenges of the modern business world. The growing amount of data available and the need to make fast, informed decisions require an integrated approach that considers D&A and BI not as separate entities, but as interconnected components of a unified analytic ecosystem. This synergy, when managed carefully and strategically, can not only improve operational efficiency, but also open up new perspectives and opportunities for businesses, allowing them to successfully navigate the vast and dynamic landscape of data and decisions.

- **Get a complete view of your data:**

  One of the main reasons to integrate D&A and BI is the ability to gain a complete and consistent view of business data. The raw data collected and analyzed through D&A forms the fundamental foundation on which BI builds its analyses and visualizations. However, the integration between these two disciplines goes far beyond just data collection and analysis. It is about transforming data into a high-value information asset, which can be exploited to make strategic decisions.

  - **Knowledge Data Transformation:**

    While D&A provides the tools to collect, clean, and analyze large volumes of data, BI focuses on transforming these analytics into actionable and understandable insights. This transformation is essential to ensure that decision-makers have all the information they need to fully understand the business context.

For example, simply knowing a drop in sales in a given quarter may be insufficient; only through integration with other data (such as customer feedback, market conditions, and competitive analysis) can BI provide a comprehensive explanation and a solid basis for corrective action.

- **Reduction of Information Silos:**
  The synergistic integration between D&A and BI helps eliminate information silos within organizations. When data and analytics are fragmented across different departments, it's difficult to get a consistent, unified view of business operations. An integrated approach allows all data sources to be combined into a single analytical platform, improving the consistency and accessibility of information and allowing an overview of business performance.

- **Make more informed decisions:**
  The ability to make informed decisions is one of the most significant competitive advantages a company can gain from integrating D&A and BI. Business Intelligence, acting as a refined filter, enriches the business context by providing decision-makers with a

deeper and more complete view of the operational landscape. This enrichment is crucial for making decisions that are not only reactive, but also proactive, based on an in-depth understanding of business and market dynamics.

- **Holistic View of Business Dynamics:** Integrating D&A with BI allows you to develop a holistic understanding of your business operations. For example, an in-depth analysis of customer buying trends, combined with operational and supply chain data, can reveal optimization opportunities that would otherwise be invisible. This broader perspective allows you to identify interconnections between various aspects of the business that can be leveraged to improve efficiency and reduce costs.

- **Support for Strategic Choices:** Strategic decisions, such as entering new markets or launching new products, require robust analytical support. The synergy between D&A and BI provides a solid foundation for such decisions, offering a combination of predictive analytics and scenario assessments that allow executives to anticipate the consequences of their choices and minimize the associated risks.

- **Improve business performance:**

The integration between D&A and BI is not limited to improving decision-making; It also has a direct impact on overall business performance. Well-thought-out decisions, based on accurate and timely information, positively affect various operational aspects, contributing to an overall improvement in performance.

  - **Operations Optimization:**

    An integrated approach allows you to accurately identify areas for improvement within your organization. For example, analyzing production data and integrating it with market demand information can lead to more effective production planning, reducing downtime and minimizing waste. This type of optimization is critical to improving productivity and keeping operating costs under control.

  - **Improved Customer Experience:**

    The ability to integrate customer feedback, sales data, and market analytics through a unified platform enables companies to deliver a more personalized and responsive customer experience. Improving the customer experience not only increases customer satisfaction and loyalty, but it can also result in a sustainable competitive advantage, as satisfied customers tend to be more loyal and generate positive word-of-mouth.

- **Sustainability of Success:**
The synergistic integration between D&A and BI positions the organization on a trajectory of long-term sustainable success. Companies that can harness the full potential of data to make informed decisions and optimize operations are better positioned to quickly adapt to market changes, innovate effectively, and maintain a competitive edge over competitors.

History of perimeters

Business Intelligence is becoming one of the main guidelines that indicates the useful path through the vastness of corporate data, transforming information into an essential strategic lever for success, but how did we get to this?

The origins of Business Intelligence

To fully understand the transformative impact of Business Intelligence in today's business context, it is crucial to retrace its historical roots.

BI, now synonymous with advanced analytics, data visualization, and decision support, had humble beginnings, developing progressively in response to the growing needs for enterprise information management and analysis. This evolutionary path has been marked by a series of technical and methodological innovations, which have laid the foundations for modern BI solutions.

The 60s and 70s: The era of reporting systems

In the pre-digital period of the 1960s and 1970s, businesses began to perceive the growing importance of information management to drive their operations. In a context where data was still relatively scarce and information systems rudimentary, Business Intelligence began to take shape through the implementation of static reporting systems. These systems were designed to generate periodic or ad hoc reports, providing a synthetic representation of company performance on a time basis.

- **Features of Reporting Systems:**
  Reporting systems at that time were limited by available technology and a lack of centralized data. The tools used were mostly based on rudimentary databases and required significant manual resources for processing and producing reports. Despite these limitations, these systems represented a critical first

step towards greater awareness and understanding of business performance. The ability to produce regular, standardized, yet static, reports provided organizations with an initial view of how their operations and financial activities were performing.

- **The Role of Manual Skills:**
  In an era when automation was minimal, reporting processes were heavily manual, requiring direct intervention from analysts to collect, verify, and interpret data. Not only did this limit the frequency and accuracy of reports, but it also made it difficult to respond promptly to market changes or emerging business needs.

The 80s: The era of data warehousing

The evolution of Business Intelligence underwent a significant acceleration in the 80s with the introduction of the concept of *data warehousing*. This revolutionary development has enabled companies to overcome the limitations of static and fragmented reporting systems by centralizing data from different sources into a single, unified repository.

- **Data Centralization:**
  Data warehousing represented a paradigm shift in the management of corporate information. Before

the advent of data warehouses, business data was often scattered across various systems and departments, making it difficult to get a unified and consistent view of business operations. With the implementation of data warehouses, organizations were able to aggregate and standardize data from different sources (such as ERP systems, CRM, and other operational applications), improving the accessibility and reliability of information.

- **More in-depth analysis:**
The centralization of data has opened up new possibilities for analysis. Companies could now perform more accurate historical analysis, identify long-term trends, and generate strategic insights that went beyond simply monitoring day-to-day operations. This new analytical capability provided a solid foundation for the development of predictive and optimization models, which would later characterize future BI evolutions.

- **Impact on Decision-Making:**
The increased availability of accurate, centralized data led to a significant improvement in decision-making. Business decision-makers, supported by more comprehensive and detailed reports, could now

make decisions based on empirical data, reducing uncertainty and improving the effectiveness of business strategies.

The 90s: The Era of OLAP Analysis

The 90s marked a further advance in the history of Business Intelligence with the introduction of OLAP (**O**nLine **A**nalytical **P**rocessing) analysis.

This new analytical approach fundamentally transformed the way companies interacted with data, moving from a static view to a dynamic, multidimensional one.

- **Multidimensional Cubes:**

  OLAP analysis introduced the concept of multidimensional cubes, which allowed data to be organized into structures that facilitated interactive exploration and analysis from different perspectives. Unlike traditional two-dimensional reports, OLAP cubes allowed decision-makers to "slice" and "slice" data according to multiple dimensions (e.g., time, geography, product), offering a deeper and more detailed understanding of the underlying relationships and trends.

- **Interactive Query:**

  With the advent of OLAP analysis, business decision-makers were no longer constrained by predefined reports. They could now explore data interactively, formulating ad-hoc queries to answer specific questions or investigate anomalies in the data. This level of interactivity was a significant step forward from traditional reporting systems, allowing for greater flexibility and speed in decision-making.

- **Complete Business View:**
  OLAP analysis allowed organizations to gain a more complete and integrated view of their business. They could simultaneously analyze financial, operational, and market data, identifying emerging trends and causal relationships that would have remained hidden with previous technologies. This multidimensional approach provided a powerful tool for strategic planning and risk management, contributing to an overall improvement in business performance.

The evolution of Data & Analytics concepts

The evolution of the concepts of Data & Analytics and Business Intelligence represents a continuous and dynamic path, closely linked to technological advancement and the growing needs of companies to compete in an increasingly complex and digital context. This evolution is not simply a chronological sequence of technological advancements, but a paradigm shift in the way organizations conceive and use data as strategic assets. The ability to effectively integrate D&A and BI translates into a significant competitive advantage, allowing companies to transform raw data into valuable insights and, ultimately, strategic actions.

- **The new millennium: the era of predictive analytics and artificial intelligence**

  With the advent of the twenty-first century, the data landscape has changed dramatically. The explosion of unstructured data—from sources such as social media, IoT sensors, and mobile devices—has rendered traditional data management and analytics approaches obsolete. At the same time, cloud computing has revolutionized the ability of organizations to store and process large volumes of data in a scalable and efficient way. In this context, predictive analytics and artificial intelligence (AI) have emerged as fundamental pillars of modern BI, opening up new possibilities for innovation and optimization of decision-making processes.

- **Automate data analysis:**
  The introduction of AI into D&A practices has enabled organizations to automate data analysis on an unprecedented scale. Machine learning models can quickly analyze large datasets, identifying hidden patterns, complex correlations, and emerging trends that would be difficult to detect with traditional methods. This automation capability significantly reduces response times, allowing companies to react in a more agile and informed way to market changes.

- **Improve forecast accuracy:**
  With advanced predictive models, organizations can more accurately anticipate market dynamics, customer needs, and operational risks. For example, more accurate demand forecasts allow you to optimize inventory management, reducing costs and improving customer satisfaction. Similarly, the ability to predict economic trends or regulatory changes allows companies to proactively adjust their strategies, minimizing exposure to risks.

- **Create new business models:**

  AI not only improves existing processes, but can also enable the creation of new business models. AI-derived insights can suggest radical innovations, such as introducing personalized products and services, transforming pricing models, or adopting entirely new *go-to-market* strategies. In an increasingly data-driven economy, the ability to leverage AI to innovate has become a critical factor for long-term success.

- **The impact of artificial intelligence on BI**

  The integration of AI into BI platforms is profoundly transforming the way companies manage and interpret data. AI technologies not only increase the efficiency and scalability of BI operations, but also their ability to generate value through automation, personalization, and risk mitigation.

  - **Automation:**

    The automation offered by AI in BI allows you to drastically reduce manual workload, increasing productivity and reducing human error. For example, AI-powered BI systems can perform real-time analysis, generate reports automatically, and even make strategic recommendations without the need for constant human intervention. This frees up human resources that can be redirected towards higher value-added activities, such as innovation and strategic planning.

- **Customization:**

  Intelligent AI-powered systems can tailor analytics to the specific needs of users, delivering more relevant and timely insights. Thanks to AI, BI platforms can learn from user interactions, optimizing the presentation of data and customizing dashboards to answer the most pressing and strategic questions of each decision-maker. This level of customization makes BI an even more powerful tool, as it allows you to make informed decisions quickly and efficiently.

- **Anomaly detection:**

  Another crucial aspect of AI applied to BI is the ability to automatically detect anomalies in data. This feature is particularly useful for preventing fraud, managing financial and operational risks, and monitoring regulatory compliance. AI can analyze vast data sets in real-time, identifying deviations from normal patterns that could indicate potential problems, such as internal fraud, errors in processes, or sudden changes in market conditions.

- **The benefits of integrating D&A and BI**

  The synergistic integration between D&A and BI offers numerous advantages that, if effectively exploited, can radically transform business performance.

  - **Comprehensive view of data:**

    BI leverages data analytics to provide a detailed and in-depth view of business performance, going beyond simply collecting and presenting information. This approach allows organizations to better understand the operating environment, identify opportunities for improvement and innovation, and more effectively monitor market and competitive dynamics.

  - **Decision-making efficiency:**

    Decisions based on accurate and timely information allow companies to respond quickly to market changes and optimize resources. The integration of D&A and BI ensures that the necessary information is available at the right time and in the most useful format, reducing decision-making time and improving the quality of strategic choices.

- **Cost reduction:**
  The automation of analytical processes and the optimization of operations, made possible by the integration of D&A and BI, help reduce overall operational costs. Companies can reduce waste, improve operational efficiency, and at the same time, invest resources in strategic areas that offer a greater return on investment.

- **Success factors for BI**
  To get the most benefit from BI, it's essential to consider a few key factors that can determine the success or failure of these initiatives.

  - **Quality data**:
    Data quality is the foundation of any BI initiative. Accurate, complete, and timely data is essential to ensure that analytics are precise and useful. Investing in data

management systems that ensure information integrity and security is critical to BI success.

- **Analytical skills**:
  The analytical competence of the staff is another crucial factor. Even the most advanced BI systems require users who are able to correctly interpret data and use insights effectively. Continuous training and updating of analytical skills are essential to maintain competitive advantage.

- **Data-driven company culture**:
  Finally, a company culture that values analysis and the strategic use of data is crucial. Companies must foster an environment in which data is seen as a strategic asset and in which all decisions, from the most operational to the most strategic, are guided by rigorous and evidence-based analysis.

BI e D&A users

Let's get to the heart of the practical applications of D&A and BI by exploring the industries that are taking full advantage of these technologies and the job roles that play a crucial role in using D&A.

Industries that leverage BI

Business Intelligence is a versatile resource, applicable in various industrial sectors, where it offers significant contributions in terms of operational efficiency, decision-making capacity and market competitiveness:

- **Financial Sector:**

  In the financial domain, banking institutions and investment firms recognize BI as a key strategic ally. Advanced financial data analytics not only allows you to monitor economic performance in real time, but also to identify emerging patterns and predict possible future scenarios. This level of insight allows organizations to develop financial strategies based on evidence, improving risk management and optimizing the investment portfolio. In addition, BI facilitates regulatory compliance, which is crucial in the industry, through the production of accurate and timely reports that comply with stringent financial industry regulations.

- **Production Sector:**

  Manufacturing companies use BI as a tool to monitor and improve their supply chain, optimize production processes, and reduce operational costs. The ability to analyze real-time data from different stages of the manufacturing process allows you to identify inefficiencies and quickly implement corrective solutions. BI also supports production planning through accurate forecasting based on market demand, helping to reduce the risk of overproduction or stockouts. This data-driven approach ensures greater flexibility and responsiveness in a global market characterized by changing and increasingly competitive dynamics.

- **Sales & Marketing:**

In the context of sales and marketing, BI proves to be an enabler for the implementation of highly personalized and targeted strategies. By collecting and analyzing customer behavioral data, companies can segment their audience in much more detail and develop marketing campaigns that precisely address the specific needs of each segment. The effectiveness of these campaigns is enhanced by BI tools that monitor performance metrics in real time, allowing for quick and targeted adjustments. In addition, BI fosters customer loyalty through the construction of personalized relationships based on a deep understanding of customer preferences and behaviors.

- **Customer Support:**

In customer service, data analytics plays a crucial role in identifying emerging issues early and proactively managing customer interactions. BI platforms allow companies to constantly monitor customer feedback, identifying recurring patterns that could indicate systemic problems or opportunities for improvement. This approach not only improves the quality of the service offered, but also helps to reduce the churn rate, keeping customer satisfaction high. In addition, BI facilitates the personalization of support, allowing agents to provide more targeted and relevant responses, improving the overall efficiency of customer service.

- **Healthcare:**

In healthcare, BI is transforming the way clinical and operational data is managed, contributing to the overall improvement of the quality of care. BI tools allow you to analyze vast volumes of data from electronic health records (EHRs), hospital management systems, and external sources such as clinical trials and public databases. This advanced analytics supports clinicians and healthcare administrators in making informed decisions, from early detection to care planning and resource management. Integrating BI into healthcare processes not only improves operational efficiency while reducing costs, but also eases the transition to more personalized, patient-centered care models, helping to reduce medical errors and improve clinical outcomes.

- **Retail and Distribution Sector:**

  In the retail industry, BI is used to optimize inventory management, improve the customer experience, and boost sales. The analysis of sales data, combined with information on purchasing behavior, allows you to predict future trends, optimize the assortment of products and improve stock management. In addition, BI helps retailers develop dynamic pricing strategies, adjusting prices in real-time based on variables such as demand, competition, and market conditions. These applications help create a smoother and more personalized shopping experience, increasing customer satisfaction and business profitability.

- **Telecommunications Sector:**

  Telcos rely on BI to manage large volumes of data generated by their networks and customer interactions. BI is used to improve network management, optimize operations, and prevent fraud. Real-time data analysis allows you to quickly identify any network issues and respond with timely interventions, minimizing downtime. In addition, BI supports customer segmentation and the development of personalized offers, helping to improve customer retention and reduce churn rates.

D&A Job Roles

The adoption of Data & Analytics requires the involvement of a diverse team of professionals, each with specific skills and responsibilities in the business decision-making process.

These roles, while distinct, are interconnected and work together to transform data into actionable insights that drive business decisions:

- **Business Managers and Leaders**:
  Business managers and leaders use information from D&A and BI to inform business strategy, like captains steering a ship through ever-changing waters. Their ability to discern patterns, trends and future prospects is crucial to successfully navigate an economic environment characterized by high uncertainty and competition. They use data to assess the effectiveness of strategies in place, identify growth opportunities, mitigate risks, and make informed decisions about investment, expansion, and innovation. This role requires a deep

understanding not only of data, but also of market dynamics and the peculiarities of the industry in which the company operates.

- **Business Analyst:**

Business Analysts play a fundamental role as a link between data and strategic decision-makers. With deep expertise in interpreting data, these professionals are able to identify significant trends, extrapolate key insights, and communicate them in a clear and understandable way to business managers. Business analysts translate complex data into stories that can guide strategic decisions, making crucial information accessible to various business stakeholders. Their work is not limited to simple analysis, but also includes data modeling, predicting future scenarios, and advising on how to make the most of information assets to gain competitive advantages.

- **D&A Experts:**

Data & Analytics experts, often known as Data Scientists, Data Engineers or Data Analysts, are the technical heart of the process of transforming raw data into useful information. These professionals use a wide range of advanced tools, such as machine learning, artificial intelligence, and advanced statistics techniques, to extract, clean, analyze, and interpret large volumes of data. Their work is essential to ensure the quality, consistency and relevance of the information that is used in decision-making processes. D&A experts must possess both technological and statistical expertise, as well as an in-depth understanding of the business environment in which they operate, in order to be able to provide innovative, data-driven solutions to the company's complex challenges.

- **IT managers:**

IT Managers play a crucial role in maintaining the technological infrastructures that support D&A operations. Their primary responsibility is to ensure that IT systems are secure, accessible, and capable of processing large amounts of data efficiently. This includes managing databases, servers, networks, and software applications, as well as protecting corporate information through advanced cybersecurity strategies. IT managers need to ensure that D&A platforms are scalable and resilient, thus supporting the growing needs of data processing. Additionally, they are responsible for data governance, which includes compliance with privacy regulations and data quality management, ensuring that the information on which business decisions are based is accurate and reliable.

- **Data Governance Officer:**

  An emerging and increasingly crucial role within organizations that adopt D&A is that of the Data Governance Officer (DGO). This professional is responsible for defining and implementing data governance policies, which include quality management, security, access, and regulatory compliance. The DGO works closely with IT Managers, D&A experts and business leaders to ensure that data is managed as a strategic asset, optimizing the use of information and minimizing associated risks. Its function is crucial to creating an environment in which data can be used securely, efficiently, and in compliance with applicable laws.

The synergy between these roles is critical to the success of data and analytics initiatives. Each professional, with their specific skills, contributes to an integrated ecosystem where data is collected, processed, analyzed and finally used to make strategic decisions. The ability to collaborate and communicate effectively across these roles is what allows organizations to harness the full potential of their data, turning it into a sustainable competitive advantage.

The Role of End Users

In the landscape of Data & Analytics and Business Intelligence technologies, end users play a crucial role that goes beyond the simple consumption of analytical results. These individuals, distributed on different organizational levels, not only interact directly with BI tools, but are also an integral part of the data enhancement process.
They contribute to the extraction of meaningful information that feeds into decision-making, making data not just a product, but a living, interactive resource within the company:

- **Line users:**
  Line users, often involved in operational roles within various departments such as sales, marketing, manufacturing, and logistics, represent the first line of interaction with BI. Through the use of reports, dashboards and ad hoc analysis tools, these users access specific and contextualized information that is directly relevant to their daily tasks. Their interaction with BI is typically geared toward solving immediate

operational problems, such as optimizing inventory, identifying sales opportunities, or managing marketing campaigns. In this context, BI serves as a tactical decision-making tool, which allows operational challenges to be responded to promptly, contributing to the achievement of organizational objectives and the continuous improvement of operational efficiency.

- **Executives and Decision Makers:**
  Executives and decision makers operate at a higher level than line users, focusing on a global and strategic vision of the company. Their interaction with BI tools focuses on analyzing macroeconomic trends, monitoring business performance against strategic objectives, and identifying opportunities for growth and innovation. Through detailed reports, advanced analytics, and predictive models, these users are able to assess the impact of long-term decisions, ensuring that the company remains competitive and aligned with its mission. BI, in this context, becomes a tool for strategic planning, risk mitigation and the continuous evaluation of business progress.

- **Customers and Partners:**
  The inclusion of customers and partners in the D&A

ecosystem represents a significant shift towards greater transparency and collaboration. Thanks to controlled access to key information, these external stakeholders can interact more effectively with the company, actively participating in the decision-making process and co-creation of value. For example, customers can monitor the status of orders, access customized reports on their consumption or performance, while partners can synchronize in real time with business operations, improving coordination and reducing response times. This openness not only strengthens business relationships, but also allows for the creation of a collaborative ecosystem in which information sharing becomes a competitive advantage.

It is important to remember:

- **The importance of collaboration:**
  The complexity of modern business challenges requires close and synergistic collaboration between all actors involved in the D&A process. End users, although they operate at different levels of the organization, must work in harmony to maximize the effectiveness of BI technologies. This implies a constant sharing of skills and knowledge, as well as

the integration of different perspectives to address complex problems holistically. The ability to build bridges between departments and foster a collaborative culture is essential to unlocking the full potential of D&A, ensuring that information is used consistently and strategically.

- **The role of corporate culture**:

In an environment where data is considered a strategic asset, company culture plays a critical role in determining the success of D&A initiatives. A context that values the centrality of data promotes the active sharing of information, transparency in decision-making processes and an informed use of analytical resources. Corporate culture then becomes the fertile ground in which data-driven practices can take root and thrive. This culture fosters not only the adoption of D&A, but also the continuous evolution of the skills and technologies needed to keep the company competitive over the long term.

- **The challenges of implementing D&A:**

Implementing D&A within an organization can present several challenges, requiring a careful and well-planned approach. Data quality is a major concern: inaccurate or incomplete data can compromise the reliability of analyses and lead to incorrect decisions. Therefore, it is essential to have rigorous data governance and data cleansing processes in place to ensure the integrity of the information used. Another significant challenge is the skills needed to effectively use D&A tools. It is essential that staff have the appropriate skills, through continuous training and updating, to fully exploit the potential of these technologies. In addition, the predisposition to change is crucial: the company's orientation towards innovation and the adoption of new paradigms is vital to overcome internal resistance and to successfully achieve the integration of D&A into the organization.

The Role of Datascientists

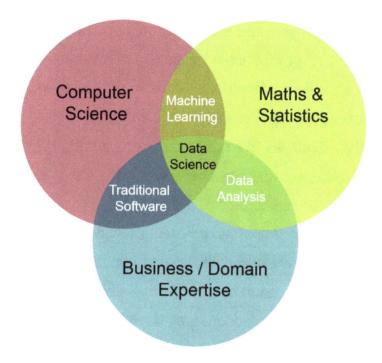

In a landscape where data represents an invaluable resource for organizations, forming the basis for strategic decisions, innovation and competitive advantages, Data Scientists emerge as key figures, equipped with the skills necessary to explore, analyze and interpret the vast flows of data that characterize the digital age.

Their role is not limited to simple analysis; they are responsible for transforming raw data into actionable insights that can guide business strategies and help achieve organizational goals. Today, more than ever, challenges are highlighted in this area:

- **The lack of skills:**

  The growing awareness of the strategic value of data has led to an exponential increase in the demand for Data Scientists, professionals capable of mastering advanced analysis techniques and applying predictive models to solve complex problems. However, the current labor market is characterized by a significant shortage of skilled talent in this sector. This lack of skills represents a significant challenge for organizations, which often find themselves forced to compete with each other to attract the few professionals available. Faced with this situation, many companies invest in in-house training programs, collaborate with academic institutions to develop specialized courses, or try to attract talent from other related fields, in an attempt to bridge the skills gap between supply and demand.

- **Data Complexity:**

  As the amount and variety of data available has increased, the complexity of the datasets that Data Scientists have to work with has grown exponentially. Data comes from a multitude of heterogeneous sources today, including not only structured databases, but also unstructured data from social media, IoT sensors, images, and videos. This requires Data Scientists not only to have solid expertise in statistics and mathematics, but also a deep understanding of big data technologies, data integration tools, and machine learning algorithms. The ability to manage, analyze, and interpret this complex data is critical to extracting valuable insights that can be used to improve decision-making processes and drive innovation.

- **Need to communicate effectively:**
One of the most significant challenges for Data Scientists is the ability to effectively communicate the results of analyses. It is not enough to be able to develop complex analytical models; It is equally important to be able to translate the results into a language that is understandable to those who do not have a technical background. This "data storytelling" skill is crucial, especially when Data Scientists interact with decision-makers and business stakeholders. Stakeholders must be able to understand insights from data analysis to make informed decisions that can influence the strategic direction of the business. The ability to simplify

complex concepts without losing the accuracy of information is an indispensable skill for the success of a Data Scientist.

- **Continuous training and interdisciplinary collaboration:**

  In an ever-changing environment, Data Scientists must engage in continuous training. Analytical technologies and methodologies evolve rapidly, and this requires constant updating of skills. Continuing education is not only about acquiring new technologies, but also about deepening knowledge in emerging areas such as artificial intelligence, blockchain, and predictive analytics. In addition, interdisciplinary collaboration is critical to the success of D&A initiatives. Data scientists must work closely with domain experts, software engineers, business analysts, and other specialists to integrate diverse perspectives, improve the accuracy of analytics, and maximize the value of data.

- **Data Scientists in Future of Organizations:**

  Looking to the future, the role of Data Scientists in organizations is destined to become increasingly strategic. As digital transformation advances, the ability to innovate and drive the adoption of new data-driven technologies will be critical to maintaining competitiveness in the marketplace. Data scientists will not only help optimize existing business processes, but will also play a key role in developing new business opportunities based on data analysis. Companies that can attract and retain this talent will be better positioned to harness the full potential of data, turning it into real, sustainable benefits over time.

Definition and skills of Datascientists

To fully understand the role of Data Scientists, it is essential to outline the distinctive characteristics and key skills that make these professionals indispensable figures in today's business landscape. Data Scientists are highly qualified specialists, whose work is based on a unique combination of multidisciplinary skills spanning mathematics, statistics, programming, and a deep knowledge of the relevant field. Their primary mission is to process, analyze, and interpret raw data through the application of advanced algorithms and predictive models, transforming complex information into meaningful, actionable insights.

Let's take a closer look at the key competencies that

distinguish them:

- **Statistical analysis:**

  Statistical analysis is one of the fundamental skills for Data Scientists. It allows them to identify patterns, correlations, and trends within the data, providing a detailed picture of the underlying dynamics that affect the business. Using advanced statistical techniques, such as regression, time series analysis, and classification, data scientists are able to discern meaningful signals in a vast volume of data, often characterized by considerable variability. This capability is crucial for isolating key variables impacting business performance, allowing decision-makers to intervene in a timely and targeted manner.

- **Programming:**

  A solid knowledge of programming languages, such as Python, R and SQL, is essential for Data Scientists. Programming is the tool through which it is possible to implement and test analysis algorithms, manipulate complex datasets and develop scalable solutions. For example, Python offers a wide range of specialized libraries, such as Pandas for data manipulation, Scikit-learn for machine learning, and

Matplotlib for visualization, which enable data scientists to operate with efficiency and accuracy. In addition, programming facilitates the automation of repetitive processes, reducing the risk of manual errors and increasing productivity.

- **Machine Learning:**

Machine learning skills are a central pillar in a Data Scientist's repertoire. Machine learning makes it possible to develop predictive models that learn from historical data to make accurate predictions about future scenarios. This is particularly relevant in business contexts where it is crucial to anticipate market trends, customer behavior, or operational anomalies. Techniques such as clustering, neural networks, and supervised and unsupervised classification algorithms allow data scientists to extract latent information from data that would otherwise be inaccessible with traditional methods.

- **Data Visualization:**

Data visualization is an equally crucial skill for data scientists, as it allows them to translate complex results into understandable and intuitive graphical representations. Tools such as Tableau, Power BI, and D3.js are commonly used to create interactive dashboards and dynamic charts that make it easier for non-experts to interpret the data. The ability to present data in a visually appealing and clear way not only makes insights more accessible, but is also critical for influencing and guiding strategic decisions within the organization.

In addition to technical skills, Data Scientists must possess soft skills that amplify their effectiveness within the organization. One of these is the ability to communicate the results of the analyses clearly and persuasively. This requires a high level of mastery of "data storytelling", which allows complex concepts to be translated into a language that is understandable and relevant to those who are not specialized in the field. The ability to communicate effectively is critical to ensuring that the insights generated are not only understood, but also used appropriately by business decision-makers.

Another crucial aspect is the propensity for interdisciplinary collaboration: the challenges and opportunities related to data often require a synergistic approach involving different skills and perspectives.
Data scientists must work closely with domain experts, software engineers, business analysts, and other stakeholders to integrate data into the operational and

strategic context of the business. This collaboration not only facilitates the implementation of data-driven solutions, but also fosters a data-driven corporate culture, where decisions are supported by empirical evidence and rigorous analysis.

The importance of Data scientists in decision-making

Data scientists have now established themselves as key figures within organizations, thanks to their ability to transform huge amounts of data into useful and strategic information for decision-making. Their influence extends beyond simple technical analysis, positioning them as real strategic consultants, capable of guiding business choices through empirical evidence and accurate forecasts.

- **Pioneering analysis for a deep understanding of the market and customers**
  Data Scientists open up new perspectives in the analysis of the market and consumer behaviors, using advanced techniques such as predictive analytics and machine learning. These professionals are able to decipher complex patterns and provide detailed insights into customer behaviors and

preferences, which become the basis for highly personalized marketing strategies. With refined audience segmentation, businesses can develop tailored offerings, improve the customer experience, and significantly increase loyalty. In a competitive environment, this ability to anticipate market needs allows companies to maintain a lasting competitive advantage.

- **Identify new business opportunities through data analysis**

  Data scientists play a crucial role in identifying new opportunities for growth and expansion for companies. Through the analysis of emerging trends and the use of predictive models, they are able to anticipate market changes and suggest new strategic directions. This proactive ability allows companies to position themselves ahead of their competitors by exploring new markets or developing innovative products. By reducing the uncertainty associated with new initiatives, Data Scientists help organizations make informed decisions, mitigate risks and maximize opportunities for success.

- **Process optimization and cost reduction**

  The optimization of business processes is another area in which Data Scientists demonstrate their strategic value. By analyzing operational workflows and applying predictive algorithms, they identify inefficiencies and propose solutions to improve asset management. Optimizing supply chains, for example, makes it possible to predict and prevent disruptions, reducing operating costs and improving the quality of the product or service offered. These interventions not only generate significant savings, but also help to strengthen the company's competitiveness, ensuring greater customer satisfaction and a solid reputation in the market.

- **Increased operational efficiency for greater competitiveness**

  Data scientists play a critical role in increasing the operational efficiency of organizations. Through in-depth analysis of operational data, they identify critical areas that require optimization and propose solutions based on concrete data. The implementation of these solutions leads to increased productivity and reduced response times to market fluctuations. The use of advanced technologies, such as real-time analytics, allows companies to quickly adapt to changes in supply and demand, optimizing logistics and ensuring a stronger competitive position. In a dynamic environment, the ability to react quickly to emerging challenges is crucial to maintaining competitiveness and sustaining long-term growth.

Innovation architect

A data scientist's ability to translate complex data sets into practical and strategic solutions allows them to improve operational efficiency, anticipate market changes, and create exceptional customer experiences.

This influence spans multiple business areas, turning analytical expertise into a key strategic lever for growth and competitiveness.

- **Development of Predictive Models for Anticipating Trends and Opportunities**

   One of the distinctive elements of the contribution of Data Scientists is the creation of advanced predictive models, capable of anticipating trends and identifying new business opportunities. Through the in-depth analysis of historical data and the application of sophisticated machine learning algorithms, these professionals develop tools that predict future consumer behaviors and market dynamics. These models act not only as a decision support in the present, but also as a strategic guide for the future, orienting the company towards potentially unexplored opportunities. For example, the ability to accurately forecast demand allows companies to optimize inventory management and calibrate production, thus avoiding costly surpluses or shortages. In addition, anticipating market trends allows companies to position themselves as leaders, launching innovations ahead of competitors and gaining significant market share.

- **Business Process Optimization to Maximize Efficiency**

  L'ottimizzazione dei processi aziendali rappresenta un altro aspetto cruciale dell'innovazione guidata dai Data Scientist. Attraverso un'analisi dettagliata dei dati operativi, essi sono in grado di identificare inefficienze e proporre soluzioni che ottimizzano la catena di produzione e distribuzione. Il loro obiettivo è quello di massimizzare l'efficienza operativa, riducendo tempi di produzione, costi associati e sprechi. Questo non solo aumenta la produttività, ma può diventare un importante vantaggio competitivo. Ad esempio, con l'implementazione di processi di automazione e digitalizzazione, le aziende possono ridurre significativamente i tempi di ciclo, migliorare la qualità del prodotto e rispondere in modo più rapido e flessibile alle richieste del mercato. In un panorama industriale sempre più competitivo, tale capacità di ottimizzazione permette alle aziende di distinguersi e mantenere una posizione di leadership.

- **Creating New Customer Experiences Through Data Analytics**

  Another area in which Data Scientists demonstrate their strategic importance is in the creation of innovative and personalized customer experiences. By analyzing a vast set of data, ranging from customer feedback to online browsing behaviors to social media interactions, data scientists can identify new ways to personalize and improve customer interaction. This translates into tailor-made offers and services, targeted promotions and engagement strategies that strengthen the relationship with the customer, increasing customer loyalty. The ability to adapt the offer to the specific needs of each customer, based on detailed data analysis, makes the company more responsive and able to meet the ever-changing expectations of the market. In this way, every interaction becomes an opportunity to consolidate the relationship with the customer and strengthen the company's competitive position.

BI tools

In this chapter, we will consider tools that enable managers to translate complex data into clear information and tangible actions.

While you may not be tech-savvy, you'll learn how these tools can become your strategic allies in making informed decisions for business success.

Popular BI tools

The landscape of Business Intelligence tools is constantly expanding, reflecting evolving business needs and the increasing complexity of data.

By looking at some of the main BI tools, we can grasp their distinctive features and the contribution they make to business decision-making:

- **Tableau:**

  Tableau is renown as one of the most powerful and versatile tools for data visualization. Its strength lies in its ability to transform complex data into intuitive visualizations, making it easy for even novice users to explore and interpret data. Tableau allows you to create interactive dashboards that enable dynamic data exploration, helping users identify patterns, trends, and correlations in a visual and immediate way. One particularly beneficial aspect of Tableau is its flexibility in integrating with a wide range of data sources, from traditional databases to big data, making it suitable for environments with data heterogeneity. In addition, the active user community and extensive availability of training resources help make Tableau an accessible and powerful tool for the entire organization.

- **Power BI:**

  Power BI, developed by Microsoft, is a tool that combines ease of use and advanced capabilities, making data analysis accessible even for users with limited technical skills. One of the strengths of Power BI is its native integration with the Microsoft ecosystem, including Excel, Azure, and SharePoint, which makes it easy to adopt within organizations already built on these technologies. Power BI allows you to create interactive reports and dashboards that can be shared in real time, supporting effective collaboration within teams. In addition to basic functionality, Power BI offers advanced analytics tools, including artificial intelligence, that enable predictive and optimization analysis. Its ability to scale with the organization makes it an ideal choice for growing businesses looking for a flexible and scalable BI solution.

- **QlikView/Qlik Sense:**

  QlikView and Qlik Sense, developed by Qlik, represent a family of BI tools based on a "discovery-driven analytics" approach. This approach allows users to explore data interactively and discover patterns and connections without having to predefine specific questions. QlikView is known for its flexibility and power in associative analysis, allowing you to freely explore connections between data and uncover hidden insights. Qlik Sense, on the other hand, offers an even more customizable user experience and an intuitive interface, making it easier for even novice users to access data. Both tools are capable of handling large volumes of data and performing real-time analytics, making them ideal for quick and informed business decisions. Qlik's innovative approach to enabling free data exploration facilitates a deeper understanding of business dynamics and the discovery of hidden opportunities.

- **MicroStrategy:**

MicroStrategy is a comprehensive and robust BI platform known for its versatility and advanced features. In addition to offering interactive reporting and dashboards, MicroStrategy supports big data integration and predictive analytics, making it a reliable choice for companies looking for a scalable and secure solution. MicroStrategy's advanced capabilities, such as in-memory analysis and sophisticated visualization, are particularly useful for strategic planning and optimization of business operations. The platform is also renowned for its robust security measures, which ensure a high level of data protection, which is crucial for businesses operating in regulated industries. The platform's scalability makes it easy to adapt to the needs of organizations of different sizes, making MicroStrategy an enterprise-grade BI solution.

These Business Intelligence tools represent only a part of the vast ecosystem of solutions available on the market. Each tool has its own unique features, benefits, and potential applications, and choosing the right solution depends on your specific business needs.

Factors such as the complexity of the data, the level of technical expertise of the users, the available budget, and the need for scalability must be carefully evaluated. In addition, in many situations, a hybrid approach, integrating multiple BI tools, can offer greater flexibility and analytical capacity, allowing the company to make the most of the data available.

Investing in effective BI tools is essential for maintaining a competitive edge, reacting quickly to market changes, and staying ahead of emerging trends.

Innovation as a driver of success

Innovation is one of the fundamental pillars that support and fuel the success of Business Intelligence tools, transforming the way organizations not only understand, but actively exploit the data available to them.

The evolution of these tools is an ongoing process, reflecting the dynamism of business needs and technological advancement, with the adoption of new capabilities that are constantly redefining their role within the global business landscape.

- **Predictive Analytics:**
  The integration of predictive analytics into modern BI tools is one of the most significant and advanced areas of innovation. This capability allows companies to go beyond descriptive analytics, which focuses on understanding what happened in the past, to project themselves into the future. Through the use of sophisticated algorithms, such as machine learning and advanced statistical models, predictive BI tools offer the ability to anticipate trends, predict behaviors, and identify potential future opportunities or risks. This forward-looking perspective transforms data into a strategic asset, allowing companies to

develop strategies based on probable future scenarios, thus improving decision-making readiness and the ability to adapt to changing market dynamics.

- **Artificial intelligence:**
  Artificial intelligence (AI) is revolutionizing the way BI tools operate, adding a new level of depth and complexity to data analytics. Through the adoption of advanced techniques such as machine learning, deep learning, and natural language processing (NLP), AI-powered BI tools are able to automate complex analytical processes, improve prediction accuracy, and detect patterns that would have escaped traditional analysis. AI also makes it possible to develop analytical models that not only recognize hidden relationships between variables, but that constantly learn and improve as the available data increases. This makes BI not only a powerful analysis tool, but also a decision-making partner capable of proactively suggesting actions and strategies, based on a more sophisticated and dynamic understanding of data.

- **Accessibility and Interactivity:**
  Accessibility and interactivity have become key areas

of innovation for BI tools, with the goal of making data analytics a universal practice within organizations. While in the past the use of BI tools was primarily reserved for specialists and analysts with advanced technical skills, the increasing focus on usability has led to the development of more intuitive and interactive user interfaces. This process of democratizing data analytics allows a wider audience, including professionals from different business functions, to actively participate in the interpretation and use of data. Tools that offer interactive dashboards, dynamic visualizations, and drag-and-drop capabilities, reduce barriers to entry, and foster a data-driven company culture. Interactivity, in particular, allows users to explore data on their own, generate real-time insights, and customize their analytics without necessarily having to resort to IT support.

- **Data Security and Scalability**
Another important dimension of innovation in BI is data security and the ability to scale. With the exponential increase in the amount of data collected and analyzed by organizations, BI tools must ensure that data is protected against external threats and

that privacy is respected, especially in highly regulated industries. In addition, the architecture of these tools must be flexible enough to adapt to business growth, supporting a growing number of users and data without compromising performance.

Innovation is the engine that pushes Business Intelligence tools towards new frontiers, transforming them into increasingly sophisticated and indispensable tools for companies. Through the adoption of advanced technologies such as predictive analytics, artificial intelligence, and improved accessibility, BI tools are continually evolving to meet the growing needs of the market and to provide businesses with the insights they need to make strategic, informed decisions.

Data visualization and Reporting

These processes are essential to the success of business intelligence as they offer an effective way to interpret and communicate complex data in business environments that are increasingly geared towards analysis and informed decision-making.

Importance of Data Visualization

Data visualization plays a crucial role in business intelligence, as it allows complex data to be understood and accessible.

Through charts, maps, and other visual tools, organizations can quickly grasp trends, identify patterns, and communicate key information. The ability to transform raw numbers into images that are immediately understandable not only facilitates decision-making, but also enables more effective communication at various levels of the organization:

- **Improving comprehension:**
  Data visualization acts as an intermediary between complex information and non-specialized users, facilitating the understanding of business dynamics. Tools such as *charts*, *histograms* and *interactive dashboards* allow users to explore data in a visual and intuitive way, overcoming the barriers imposed by the abstract nature of numerical data. This approach not only improves the interpretation of information, but also fosters a deeper understanding of operational and strategic dynamics. Strategically using *colors, shapes,* and *animations* in visualizations

can highlight critical aspects, ensuring that relevant details don't go unnoticed.

- **Identify patterns and trends:**

  The ability to identify *patterns* and *trends* within large volumes of data is one of the main benefits of data visualization. Through the use of interactive charts and dynamic visualizations, you can uncover correlations and anomalies that might be missed by traditional analysis. This capability is crucial for companies looking to anticipate market trends, identify growth opportunities, and prevent potential operational issues. Tools such as *heatmaps* and *cluster analysis* allow you to group similar data and visualize hidden correlations, providing a clearer and more strategic view of market and operational dynamics.

- **Effective communication:**

  Data visualization is also a powerful tool for both internal and external communication. Transforming complex data into clear and meaningful visualizations makes it easier to share insights with various stakeholders, improving collaboration and business transparency. In an enterprise environment where decisions must be made quickly, the ability to present data in visual form allows executives to immediately understand the implications of a dataset and act accordingly.

This is especially true in the context of business *presentations* and *reports*, where well-designed visualizations can enhance the persuasive impact of the message, increasing the likelihood that recommendations will be accepted and implemented.

Advanced data visualization techniques

In addition to basic practices, the use of advanced visualization techniques can further enrich the experience of interpreting data.

These techniques not only improve the accuracy and depth of analysis, but also offer new ways to engage users and promote a deeper, more intuitive understanding of information:

- **Interactive and dynamic visualization:** The interactive visualization allows users to explore data dynamically, focusing on specific details and tailoring the visualization to their needs. Using interactive dashboards and drill-down tools, users can move from a general view to more granular details, making it possible to analyze at different levels of detail.

This flexibility increases the effectiveness of personalized analysis, allowing users to quickly answer specific questions and adapt visualizations in real time to uncover new insights. Interactivity also stimulates creative exploration, encouraging users to test different hypotheses and scenarios.

- **Storytelling with Data:**

Integrating storytelling elements into data visualizations adds a narrative layer, making it easier to understand the data in a broader context. This engaging technique can make the data more memorable and meaningful to users. Data-driven storytelling combines images, text, and timelines to build a coherent narrative that guides the user through key data points. By using a narrative approach, organizations can not only communicate the results of the analyses, but also motivate specific actions. For example, a chart that shows how sales have evolved over time can be enriched with customer success stories or significant market events that have influenced trends.

- **Using multidimensional maps and charts:**
The use of multidimensional maps and graphs can provide deeper perspectives on complex data, allowing for the representation of relationships and correlations that might otherwise be missed in a one-dimensional presentation. Geographic maps, for example, allow you to visualize spatial data and identify regional patterns, such as differences in consumption between different geographic areas. Three-dimensional scatter plots or heatmaps allow multiple variables to be represented simultaneously, revealing hidden interconnections and clusters. This ability to represent multiple dimensions on a single graph allows analysts to gain a more integrated view of the data, making it easier to identify global trends and local details at the same time. The use of such techniques is particularly useful in industries such as logistics, where understanding spatial dynamics is crucial, or in marketing, where analyzing consumer preferences requires a multifaceted and detailed view.

Role of Reports and Dashboards

Reports and dashboards are the primary tools through which organizations present and communicate the results of their analyses. Their role is critical in transforming data into useful and accessible information, enabling different levels of the business to make informed decisions.

Both tools, although they have different purposes, work in synergy to offer a complete picture of business performance and dynamics.

- **Report: a detailed analysis**

  They are characterized by their ability to provide a complete and in-depth picture of information, supporting complex analyses and strategic reflections:

  - **Structured presentation:**

    They present information in a structured and organized way, facilitating a detailed understanding of the data. This presentation can include tables, charts, and textual analysis to give you a complete picture of specific business aspects. The logical and sequential structure of the reports allows users to follow a clear common thread, analyzing numerical and descriptive data with precision.

- **Deepening of critical aspects:**
Through the inclusion of detailed textual and visual analysis, the reports allow you to drill down into critical aspects of the business. This is crucial for identifying opportunities, risks, and areas for improvement. Reports provide the foundation for predictive analytics and projections, helping organizations plan strategically and mitigate risk.

- **Customization of analyses:**
The flexible structure of the reports allows the analysis to be customized according to the specific needs of the different business functions. This makes reports suitable tools for various stakeholders, from operations teams to executives. Each business function may require specific reports that highlight the metrics and performance indicators that are most relevant to their day-to-day activities and strategic goals.

- **Dashboard: A Panoramic View**
Dashboards provide an overview of business performance, playing a unique and complementary

role to reports. They offer quick and intuitive access to key information, supporting real-time monitoring and analysis:

- **Key data aggregation:**
  Dashboards aggregate key data into a single interface, giving you a comprehensive, concise view of the most relevant metrics. This visual representation makes it easy to understand the overall state of the company immediately. The use of colored graphs and indicators facilitates quick interpretation of trends and anomalies.

- **Rapid evaluation of critical metrics:**
  Thanks to their visual and intuitive structure, dashboards allow for quick evaluation of the most critical metrics. This feature is particularly useful for real-time monitoring of business performance. Managers can take immediate action in the event of deviations from targets, ensuring that corrective actions are timely and effective.

- **Early Decision Support:**
  Instant access to key data through dashboards facilitates timely decision-making.

Their design to highlight critical elements allows users to quickly focus on the most relevant aspects of the business. Dashboards can be customized for different levels of access, ensuring that the most relevant information is available to each user.

Efficient integration of Reports and Dashboards

The effectiveness of reports and dashboards emerges when they are integrated synergistically, each playing its own specific role within the bigger picture. Combining these tools allows you to gain a comprehensive and dynamic understanding of your business operations:

- **Detailed analysis and synthetic view:** Reports provide detailed and in-depth analysis, while dashboards provide a concise and at-a-glance view. Integrating both tools allows you to obtain a complete and balanced understanding of business dynamics. This integration allows organizations to operate with a clear view of the present, supported by detailed analysis of the past.

- **Decision Agility:**

    The combination of detailed reports and
    overview dashboards provides comprehensive
    decision-making support. Users can drill down
    into specific aspects through reports and, at
    the same time, evaluate the overall trend
    through dashboards. This duality allows for
    greater decision-making agility, which is
    essential in an increasingly complex and
    competitive business environment, where
    decisions must be made quickly and with
    accurate information.

Customizing Dashboards

Dashboards should be customized to the needs of end
users to maximize utility and effectiveness. Personalization
is a key element in ensuring that dashboards meet the
specific operational and decision-making needs of users.

By selecting key metrics, choosing preferred visualizations,
and configuring custom notifications, dashboards can
become powerful, tailored tools that improve productivity
and business efficiency.

- **Adapt to the specifics of the role:**
  Customizing dashboards starts by tailoring their content to the specifics of the user's role. Each role within an organization has different needs and responsibilities, so dashboards must be designed to provide relevant and crucial information for each user's day-to-day activities and specific decisions.
  E.g.:

  - *Operational Manager:*
    A customized dashboard for an operations manager could include metrics related to productivity, inventory, and the performance of the teams under their supervision.
    This dashboard could also show indicators of process efficiency, allowing the manager to identify areas for improvement and optimize daily operations.

  - *Sales Manager:*
    A dashboard adapted for a sales manager might focus on sales metrics, revenue forecasting, and customer analytics. It could include visualizations on sales trends, performance analysis by geography, and data on upsell and cross-sell opportunities.

This information enables the manager to make strategic decisions based on actionable data.

- **Interactive and customizable dashboards**: The key to customizing dashboards lies in their interactivity and level of customization. These features give users the flexibility to tailor data visualization to their needs and preferences, contributing to a better user experience and greater effectiveness in data analysis.

Features of Interactive Dashboards:

Selecting Key Metrics:

Users should be able to select the key metrics that are most relevant to their activities and interests. This allows you to focus only on performance indicators that directly affect the user's results and responsibilities, reducing the overload of unnecessary information.

- **Choice of favorite views:**
  The ability to choose from different visualizations (bar charts, maps, pie charts, etc.) allows users to tailor the visual representation of the data to their preferences. Not only does this improve the

accessibility of information, but it also helps to make the analysis more intuitive and understandable for each user, considering their visual and cognitive preferences.

- **Configuring custom notifications:** Dashboards can be customized to send automatic notifications when certain metrics reach specific thresholds, allowing users to be promptly notified of critical events. This aspect is crucial to maintain continuous and immediate control over company performance and to react quickly to situations that require timely intervention.

Data visualization and decision-making

Data visualization is not simply a decorative tool or an end in itself; It is an essential element in the context of business decision-making, acting as a bridge between data analysis and the implementation of effective strategies. The ability to transform raw data into understandable visual representations is crucial to ensure that the extracted information directly influences business decisions, contributing to the improvement of operations and the achievement of strategic objectives.

Effective data visualization acts as a catalyst in decision-making, converting complex sets of information into actionable insights. This transformation process allows business decision-makers to quickly assimilate data and use it to make informed decisions, reducing the time and effort required to understand the business reality. In a competitive context, where speed and accuracy are crucial, a clear and well-structured visualization becomes a distinctive element that can determine the success or failure of a business strategy.

- **Informed decision support:**
  Data visualization is critical to supporting business decisions based on actionable and relevant information. This support manifests itself through several key aspects:

  - **Clear and intuitive visualizations:**
    The ability to design visualizations that are easily interpreted by stakeholders is critical to ensuring that complex data is transformed into accessible information. Well-designed charts and organized tables reduce complexity and make it easy to quickly assimilate critical

information.

Effective design not only makes data more understandable, but also facilitates communication within business teams, promoting evidence-based discussions and improving the quality of collective decisions.

Selection of the relevant information:

The relevance of the data displayed is just as crucial as its clarity. Carefully choosing key metrics and indicators, aligned with business goals, ensures that the information presented is directly relevant to the decision-making context. This targeted approach not only reduces uncertainty, but also increases the effectiveness of the strategies adopted, as decision makers can rely on data that is not only accurate, but also meaningful to their specific responsibilities.

- **Performance monitoring:**

Data visualization is not limited to facilitating decision-making; It also plays a crucial role in the continuous monitoring of business performance, offering a number of strategic benefits that improve the agility and responsiveness of the organization.

- **Agility in response:**
  Access to real-time visualizations of business performance allows for an agile response to sudden changes in the market, internal evolutions or other critical variables. This ability to respond quickly is essential to maintain competitiveness in an ever-changing market environment. Companies that can adapt their strategies early on based on up-to-date data can minimize risk, take advantage of emerging opportunities, and maintain a competitive edge over less responsive competitors.

- **Quickly identify trends and anomalies:**
  Dynamic visualizations, especially those that enable interactive data exploration, are powerful tools for early identification of trends and anomalies. The ability to detect favorable trends early or flag potential problems allows decision makers to intervene before problems become critical or, conversely, to capitalize on opportunities before they are recognized by competitors. This proactivity in monitoring business performance is critical to maintaining

strict control over operations and ensuring that the company remains aligned with its strategic objectives.

- **Alignment with business goals**:

The connection between data visualization and decision-making is not only an operational element, but also a key factor for the strategic alignment of the entire organization:

- **Results-oriented analysis:**

  Data analysis that is driven by business goals ensures that the information extracted is targeted to achieve specific outcomes. This approach allows for a more effective allocation of resources and greater consistency in the decisions made, since all choices are oriented towards the achievement of long-term objectives. Using results-oriented visualizations helps keep the organization focused on the main objectives, avoiding distractions and dispersion of resources.

- **Strategic adaptability:**

  The ability to tailor data visualizations to meet current business goals allows for strategic flexibility that is essential in an ever-changing market environment. Companies can redefine their priorities in real time, focusing on specific areas that require immediate action, and steer decisions towards achieving key objectives. This dynamism not only drives operational agility, but also optimizes the path to business success, ensuring that the business remains responsive and competitive.

BI & AI/ML

The data landscape is characterized by constant change, marked by the exponential increase in the amount of data and the introduction of new types, including unstructured data.

The latter, coming from heterogeneous sources such as social media, videos, images and text, pose significant challenges for organizations, given their complexity and the difficulty of integration into traditional management systems.

In this context, advanced technologies such as Artificial Intelligence (AI) and Machine Learning (ML) are becoming increasingly indispensable for the management and analysis of complex data.

A bridge between two worlds

The shift from a world dominated by structured data, easily interpreted using conventional analytical tools, to one increasingly based on unstructured data has introduced a new dimension of complexity. Structured data, organized into predefined formats such as relational tables, continues to be critical for many applications, but the growing importance of unstructured data requires more sophisticated tools to extract value.

The complexity arising from these new forms of data lies in their heterogeneity: information from disparate sources that cannot be easily organized into a single data schema. To manage this complexity, new analytical methodologies must be adopted that go beyond conventional methods, offering solutions that can address the vast and dynamic landscape of modern data:

- **AI and ML as fundamental pillars:**
  In this context, AI and ML are emerging as central technologies for modern data management. AI's ability to autonomously learn from data and

continuously adapt to new information represents a crucial advance over traditional analytical techniques. AI is able to examine huge volumes of data, detecting patterns and trends that would otherwise be invisible to human observation. This approach goes beyond simple descriptive analysis, allowing organizations to gain a deeper understanding of the underlying dynamics.

At the same time, ML further contributes with algorithms capable of autonomously identifying hidden relationships and complex patterns. Thanks to this capability, ML unlocks enormous information potential, allowing not only to describe the phenomena observed, but also to predict future developments, an essential element for improving business decision-making.

- **The transformative role of BI integration:**
  The integration of AI and ML with Business Intelligence (BI) represents a game-changer in the way businesses analyze and use data. Traditional BI, historically used to analyze past data and provide retrospective insights, is evolving into a predictive and proactive platform. AI, for example, automates the discovery of meaningful insights, reducing the

time it takes to analyze and facilitating faster, deeper understanding. This allows companies to act quickly and dynamically adapt to an ever-changing market. At the same time, ML enhances BI's predictive capacity, allowing it to not only respond to emerging trends, but anticipate them. The adoption of these technologies transforms BI from a post-event analysis tool to a system capable of predicting future scenarios and guiding business strategies towards more targeted and informed decisions.

- **Concrete application scenarios:**
The practical applications of AI and ML in different industries are already evident and constantly expanding. In marketing, for example, AI can analyze consumer behavior through data collected from different digital platforms, making it possible to predict future purchasing trends and personalize marketing campaigns in a highly targeted way. This type of advanced analytics allows businesses to optimize resources, improving return on investment (ROI) and delivering more relevant user experiences. In the sales industry, ML can significantly improve supply chain management by predicting demand more accurately and optimizing inventory

management. The ability to accurately predict purchasing patterns helps reduce operating costs and improve overall efficiency, a key factor in business competitiveness.

- **AI and ML as discovery tools:**
  The introduction of AI and ML is not limited to the simple analysis of existing data; These technologies also expand the ability to discover new patterns, relationships, and opportunities that may be missed by human analysis. This ability to go beyond the surface of data allows organizations to gain a deeper understanding of business dynamics and capture hidden opportunities that can be crucial to success in highly competitive markets. With their ability to detect subtle correlations and complex patterns, AI and ML give businesses a competitive advantage, allowing them to respond more accurately to complex challenges and.

- **Ethical considerations and emerging issues:**
  The integration of these advanced technologies into data analytics inevitably raises ethical questions and privacy concerns. The extensive collection and analysis of data requires a careful balance between technological innovation and responsibility in

information management. Protecting privacy and securing personal data is not just a legal issue, it is an ethical imperative that companies must take seriously. Organizations must adopt strict policies that comply with existing data protection regulations, such as the GDPR, and that promote a culture of transparency and informed consent. This involves clearly communicating to users how their data is being used and taking proactive measures to ensure its security, ensuring that technological innovation does not compromise individual rights.

AI and D&A Enhancement

Artificial Intelligence represents a disruptive and transformative force in the field of data analysis, revolutionizing the processes by which organizations collect, process and use information.

With the exponential increase in the amount of data available and the increasing complexity of the information to be managed, AI stands as the technological solution capable of addressing these challenges, significantly improving every phase of the data lifecycle.

Through the application of advanced machine learning techniques and sophisticated algorithms, AI not only accelerates and automates traditional processes but also offers new forecasting and decision-making capabilities, leading to deeper understanding and more informed business decisions.

Let's see how AI acts at different stages of the data analysis process:

- **Data Extraction:**

  The data extraction phase is the fundamental starting point for any analysis process. Traditionally, extracting data from heterogeneous sources required significant human resources and carried a high risk of errors, especially when it came to managing unstructured data such as text, images, or videos. AI fundamentally transforms this process, improving its efficiency and accuracy through the use of algorithms capable of navigating through diverse data sources with unprecedented speed and accuracy. An emblematic example of this transformation is represented by Natural Language Processing (NLP) techniques, which allow the automatic extraction of relevant information from textual documents. Thanks to these techniques, AI is able to understand and interpret natural language, transforming unstructured content into structured data ready for analysis. This not only speeds up the extraction process, but also increases the completeness and accuracy of the information collected, minimizing the risk of omitting critical data.

- **Data Cleansing:**

One of the biggest challenges in the data analysis process is ensuring the quality and reliability of information. The data cleansing phase is crucial in this regard, as any error in this phase can compromise the entire analysis. AI intervenes by automating many of the tasks related to data cleansing, such as identifying and correcting errors, managing missing data, and removing duplication. Thanks to machine learning, AI is able to identify error patterns and correct them autonomously, improving data consistency and reducing the margin for human error. This automation not only elevates the quality of the data, but also frees up human resources that can be used in more strategic activities, such as designing new analyses or innovating products and services.

- **Data Preparation:**

The data preparation phase is an essential step in

ensuring that the information is ready for analysis. In this context, AI plays a critical role in automating complex tasks such as data normalization, aggregation, and transformation. AI ensures that data from different sources is standardized and integrated consistently, facilitating comparability and joint analysis. The accuracy and consistency offered by AI in data preparation are essential to avoid bias in subsequent analyses. With AI's ability to handle large amounts of data with precision, organizations can ensure that their analyses are representative of the entire data set, thereby improving the validity of the conclusions drawn.

- **Data Analysis:**
  AI's true potential in data analytics emerges in the actual analysis phase, where machine learning algorithms can explore the data in depth, identifying patterns and trends that would otherwise be invisible. This ability to uncover non-obvious insights is critical to enriching business decision-making. AI makes it possible to analyze large volumes of data in real time, detecting hidden connections and offering new perspectives that can lead to significant competitive advantages. For example, in the context

of marketing, AI can analyze consumer behaviors and suggest personalized strategies to improve customer engagement and loyalty. In sales, AI can predict demand cycles, optimizing procurement strategies and reducing operational costs.

- **Predictive models:**
  In addition to improving retrospective analysis, AI excels at developing predictive models that allow organizations to anticipate future events with a high degree of accuracy. These models are particularly useful in dynamic industries such as finance, healthcare, and manufacturing, where the ability to predict future trends and behaviors can be the difference between success and failure. For example, in the financial sector, AI can develop models that predict market fluctuations, allowing investors to make informed decisions and minimize risks. Similarly, in the manufacturing industry, AI can optimize supply chain management by predicting demand accurately, thereby improving operational efficiency and reducing storage costs.

Ethical considerations and handling AI in data analytics:

The widespread adoption of AI in data analytics is

not without significant ethical challenges. Transparency, accountability, and privacy protection have become crucial concerns that require careful and accountable management. As AI capabilities increase, organizations must address issues such as algorithmic bias, data surveillance, and respecting user privacy. It is essential for companies to implement clear policies and strict practices to ensure that the use of AI is aligned with ethical principles and that it respects the rights of individuals. This includes complying with existing regulations, such as GDPR in Europe, and taking a proactive approach that puts trust and transparency at its core. Companies must be transparent about how data is used and ensure that users have control over their personal information.

Machine Learning in BI

The combination of Artificial Intelligence and Machine Learning in Business Intelligence represents a game-changer for companies, allowing them to leverage data in increasingly sophisticated ways to make strategic decisions. This synergy is transforming the business landscape, not only by optimizing existing processes, but also by opening up new opportunities, reducing risk, and improving overall efficiency.

Below, we look at some specific applications of AI and ML in the context of BI:

- **Predictive Analytics:**

  Predictive analytics, powered by machine learning algorithms, is one of the most advanced and powerful applications of modern BI. This technology allows organizations to analyze large volumes of historical data to accurately predict future trends. In the context of sales, for example, AI can predict future sales volumes, allowing for accurate production planning and optimized inventory management. Not only does this help reduce costs related to overproduction or stock shortages, but it also improves the company's ability to respond to market fluctuations. Another critical field of application is the prediction of the churn rate, or customer churn rate. Through the analysis of behavioral and transactional data, AI algorithms can identify warning signs of customer dissatisfaction, allowing companies to intervene promptly with personalized retention strategies, such as tailored offers or improvements in customer service, thus reducing customer loss and maintaining a solid customer base.

- **Personalization of the customer experience:** The ability to personalize the customer experience has become a critical success factor for modern businesses. Machine learning plays a central role in this process, allowing companies to analyze behavioral data and user preferences in detail. Through continuous learning from the data collected, algorithms can offer highly personalized product or service recommendations, improving customer engagement and satisfaction. Platforms such as Netflix or Spotify are examples of excellence in this area. By using AI algorithms to analyze users' consumption patterns and preferences, these platforms are able to suggest content that perfectly matches individual tastes, increasing the time spent on the platform and strengthening user loyalty.

- **Fraud detection:** In the financial sector, AI has become an essential tool for fraud protection. Machine learning algorithms monitor financial transactions and user behavior in real time, identifying anomalous patterns that could indicate fraudulent activity. This continuous, proactive monitoring allows businesses to take immediate action, reducing the risk of significant financial losses and protecting customer trust. The adoption of AI solutions for fraud detection goes beyond simply identifying suspicious transactions. These systems can learn and adapt to new types of fraud as they emerge, constantly improving their effectiveness and reducing the chance of fraudulent behavior escaping detection.

- **Automation of Operational Decisions:**
AI and ML are also transforming the way operational decisions are made in companies, especially in industries such as manufacturing and logistics. With predictive analytics, organizations can automate critical decisions in real-time, such as resource allocation or inventory management, improving operational efficiency and reducing costs. In dynamic environments such as logistics, where conditions can change rapidly, the ability to adapt and react immediately to changes in demand or disruptions in the supply chain is crucial. AI provides the tools needed to anticipate these changes and adapt operations accordingly, keeping the business agile and competitive.

- **Optimization of internal processes:**
The optimization of internal business processes is

another field where AI and ML demonstrate enormous potential. In supply chain management, for example, AI can analyze data related to production, logistics, and sales to identify inefficiencies and suggest improvements. This ability to analyze and optimize complex processes leads to a reduction in operating costs and an improvement in the timeliness of deliveries.

Additionally, AI can help businesses better manage their resources, reducing waste and improving overall productivity. By analyzing data from different internal sources, algorithms can identify bottlenecks or redundant processes, providing suggestions on how to streamline operations and improve efficiency.

- **Sentiment analysis on social platforms:**
  Social media sentiment analysis is an emerging application of AI in BI, allowing businesses to understand customer opinions and emotions about a brand or product in real-time. AI algorithms analyze data from social platforms such as Twitter, Facebook, or Instagram, identifying positive, negative, or neutral sentiments expressed in users' posts and comments.

  This analytical capability allows businesses to react quickly to emerging issues, improving brand reputation and optimizing marketing strategies. For example, a company could quickly identify an emerging negative trend related to a new product and intervene with targeted communication campaigns or changes to the product itself, reducing the negative impact and improving public perception.

- **Optimization of marketing campaigns:**
AI has become an indispensable tool for optimizing marketing campaigns, especially in the context of digital advertising. By analyzing demographic, behavioral, and purchasing data, machine learning algorithms can identify the most promising audiences and optimize campaign targeting. This leads to greater accuracy in reaching the right audience with the right message, increasing the return on investment (ROI) of advertising campaigns.

AI-powered optimization is not limited to targeting. The algorithms can also determine the best time to show ads or suggest creative changes that resonate best with the target audience. These incremental improvements result in more effective ad campaigns and increased efficiency in ad spend, which directly impacts business outcomes.

Challenges and opportunities in integration

The integration of Artificial Intelligence (AI) with Business Intelligence (BI) represents a complex and promising frontier for modern companies. While it presents significant challenges, it also offers opportunities that can fundamentally transform business strategies, improving competitiveness and operational efficiency:

- **Technological complexity and specialized skills:**
  The implementation of AI and Machine within BI processes introduces considerable technological complexity. These tools require highly specialized skills that are not always readily available within organizations. The creation of a qualified team, capable of effectively managing the integration of AI and BI, becomes an imperative necessity. Such integration requires not only in-depth knowledge of data science, but also a solid understanding of business dynamics and specific operational needs. Continuous training and professional development are essential to keep staff up-to-date on the latest technologies and methodologies. The speed at which

AI and ML tools evolve makes a continuous learning approach critical. In addition, interdisciplinary collaboration between data scientists, BI experts, software engineers, and business analysts is crucial to overcome technical barriers and promote the seamless integration of different skills. This synergy between different business sectors favors the development of innovative solutions, capable of responding to the complex needs of the modern market.

- **Costs incurred by implementation:**
Implementing AI-powered BI solutions involves considerable upfront costs, which include not only purchasing cutting-edge technology but also investing in staff training and system integration. For many businesses, especially small and medium-sized enterprises (SMBs), these costs are a significant hurdle.

However, it is essential to view these investments as a long-term strategic expense rather than an immediate cost.

Companies that manage to overcome this initial hurdle can gain substantial competitive advantages. The integration of AI and BI has the potential to dramatically improve analytical capabilities, enabling more informed and precise decisions. Additionally, the resulting operational efficiency can lead to a significant return on investment, reducing long-term costs and improving overall business performance.

- **Data security:**
  The use of AI and ML in business processes involves intensive use of data, often sensitive, which raises important security issues. Protecting data from unauthorized access and complying with privacy regulations, such as GDPR in Europe, are crucial challenges. Security breaches can not only result in serious legal and financial consequences, but also irreparably damage the company's reputation.
  To address these challenges, robust data security policies must be implemented, including the adoption of advanced encryption technologies, secure access management, and ongoing staff training on data protection best practices.
  In addition, companies must be ready to respond quickly to any security incidents, with well-defined contingency plans that minimize potential damage.

At the same time, it offers a rich terrain of opportunities that can shape the future of business strategies:

- **Better decisions based on accurate information:**

  The integration of AI and BI provides an opportunity to significantly improve business decision-making. AI can analyze large amounts of data, spotting hidden patterns and providing accurate predictions that allow businesses to make more informed decisions. This data-driven approach increases the accuracy of strategic decisions, improving overall business performance and strengthening market competitiveness.

  Predictive analytics, one of the most powerful applications of AI, allows companies to anticipate market trends, optimize operations, and reduce risk. For example, AI can predict changes in demand, allowing for effective production planning and optimized inventory management, thereby reducing operating costs and improving customer satisfaction.

- **Increased efficiency through automation:**

  Another crucial benefit of integrating AI into BI is the automation of repetitive and low-value-added tasks. Thanks to AI, companies can automate many steps in the data analysis process, reducing the manual workload and freeing up human resources to focus on more strategic and creative tasks. Not only does this reduce operational costs, but it also improves the efficiency and overall productivity of the business.

Automation allows complex analyses to be performed much faster than traditional methods, improving the company's responsiveness to market dynamics. Human resources, freed from mechanical activities, can devote themselves to innovating and developing new strategies, helping to create a more dynamic and value-oriented work environment.

- **Discovering new business opportunities:**
  AI, integrated with BI, gives companies powerful tools to identify new business opportunities and personalize customer interactions. Through the analysis of customer data, AI can identify new market niches, develop innovative products and optimize marketing campaigns, adapting them to the specific needs of customers. This ability to adapt quickly to market dynamics gives companies a significant competitive advantage. For example, AI can be used to detect fraud in real-time, improve risk management, or optimize product development processes, allowing companies to stay ahead of the curve in an ever-changing market. Continuous discovery of new opportunities, fueled by advanced

data analytics, is essential to sustaining long-term growth and success.

Future prospects

The dynamic integration between Artificial Intelligence and Business Intelligence is rapidly gaining momentum, charting an evolutionary path that promises to redefine the business landscape in the coming years.

With the advancement of AI and Machine Learning technologies, this convergence is not only a current trend, but a fundamental pillar for the future of business strategies:

- **Expanding AI and ML technologies:**
  The evolution of AI and ML technologies will be a key driver for the ever-deeper integration of these capabilities into BI solutions. As new algorithms and methodologies emerge, predictive analytics will become even more precise and robust, enhancing BI as a central tool for strategic planning and operational decision support. Deep learning algorithms and reinforcement learning techniques are just a few examples of emerging technologies that promise to amplify companies' ability to predict trends, optimize processes, and proactively respond

to market dynamics.

This technological expansion will also allow BI solutions to be more scalable, allowing organizations to process and analyze increasingly large and complex volumes of data. Integrating these technologies with existing BI systems will require continuous innovation, prompting companies to invest in advanced IT infrastructure and specialized skills.

- **Strengthening advanced analytics:**

  The future of AI/ML-integrated BI is not limited to improving predictive capabilities, but promises a significant strengthening of advanced analytics. By using techniques such as multivariate analysis, advanced clustering, and nonlinear predictive modeling, companies will be able to spot not only obvious patterns in the data, but also subtle correlations and influences that might otherwise be missed. This advanced analytics capability will enable organizations to anticipate market changes, customer behaviors, and competitive dynamics, providing a significant strategic advantage more accurately. In addition, the integration of AI and ML with technologies such as real-time data analytics and the Internet of Things (IoT) will further enhance

BI, allowing companies to adapt their strategies in near real-time. Advanced analytics will thus be able to provide more granular and actionable insights, which will support timely and informed decisions in an ever-changing market environment.

- **Extensive automation and networking:** Automation is set to play an increasingly central role in the integration of AI, ML, and BI. In the future, we will see an extension of automation into complex tasks, which will not only ease the workload of analysts, but fundamentally transform the way information is collected, analyzed, and used. For example, automating data preparation—one of the most expensive steps in the BI process—could become the norm, with AI algorithms that clean, transform, and organize data autonomously, providing a solid foundation for analysis. Similarly, the automatic creation of advanced reports, based on dynamic and customizable templates, will allow users to access critical information in a faster and more intuitive way. This automation will likely also extend to autonomous management of day-to-day BI operations, where AI-powered systems will be able to constantly monitor business performance, identify anomalies, and suggest corrective actions without direct human intervention. The interconnection between different business systems, enabled by AI, will enable an integrated and consistent view of operations, improving synchronization between various departments and business processes. This level of automation and interconnection will not only improve efficiency, but also drive faster innovation and a greater ability to adapt to changing market conditions.

It is important to recognize that the integration between AI and BI does not follow a linear, predetermined path, but rather an iterative process that requires close collaboration between BI and AI teams.

This collaborative approach is essential to maximize the value of this integration, ensuring that advanced AI capabilities are synergistically integrated into the broader context of enterprise BI.

The continuous sharing of knowledge and expertise between data scientists, BI analysts, and other business stakeholders is critical to developing solutions that are not only technically advanced, but also aligned with the strategic and operational needs of the business. This interdisciplinary collaboration fosters innovation and allows emerging challenges to be addressed more effectively, ensuring that BI solutions evolve as AI and ML technologies advance.

In parallel with technological innovation, it is essential to consider the ethical implications of the use of AI and ML in BI. Transparency, fairness, and accountability in AI models must be prioritized to avoid discrimination and ensure that business decisions are fair and impartial. The increasing complexity and power of algorithms makes it even more urgent to constantly monitor automated decisions to prevent biases and unintentional discrimination.

In addition, compliance with privacy regulations and data protection must remain a central element of the integration between AI and BI. Algorithms must be designed and implemented in such a way that they strictly comply with ethical and regulatory standards, ensuring responsible use of data and protecting the rights of individuals.

Finally, continuous monitoring and adaptation of algorithms is crucial to ensure that AI-powered BI solutions remain ethically responsible and aligned with long-term business goals. This proactive approach will help build a sustainable and morally responsible future in advanced business analytics by fostering trust in AI technologies and their public acceptance.

Data Governance and Security

Effective data management serves as an essential basis for accurate analysis and informed decision-making.

This chapter focuses on the importance of data governance and security, highlighting their crucial role in business intelligence (BI). Proper data management not only supports the reliability of analytics, but is also critical to ensuring the integrity and protection of information within the organization.

Data governance in Data & Analytics strategies

Data governance is a process that goes beyond simply defining rules and guidelines. It is at the heart of the entire Data & Analytics ecosystem, ensuring that data is managed consistently, securely, and in compliance with regulations. Effective governance allows you to build solid trust in the organization's information assets, which is essential for the success of data-driven business strategies.

Let's take a closer look at how data governance helps ensure data quality, security, and regulatory compliance:

- **Ensure data quality:**
  Data quality is a critical component of successful data and analytics initiatives. Robust data governance is essential to ensure that data is accurate, consistent, and up-to-date, which is key to validating analytics and making informed business decisions.
  - **Precision:**
    Data governance is concerned with establishing strict standards and validation processes to ensure data accuracy. Accuracy

is crucial to prevent errors in the data from resulting in incorrect analysis and, consequently, poor business decisions. This involves defining methods for verifying and correcting data, as well as preventing duplication and inconsistencies.

- **Coherence:**

  Data consistency is essential to avoid ambiguity and contradictions in analytical results. Effective governance sets clear standards for data structure, formatting, and interpretation, ensuring that information is consistent and that datasets from different sources can be seamlessly integrated and analyzed. This approach reduces data variability and promotes a single version of the truth across the organization.

- **Update:**

  Data governance also involves managing the lifecycle of data, ensuring that data is constantly updated to reflect the latest operational realities. This involves establishing processes for the acquisition, transformation and regular updating of data, as well as for managing update timelines, in order to ensure that analyses are always based on current and relevant information.

- **Protect your data from unauthorized access:** In a context where the amount of sensitive data managed by organizations is constantly growing, data governance plays a crucial role in protecting information from unauthorized access and undue manipulation. This is essential not only to prevent security breaches, but also to maintain stakeholder trust and regulatory compliance.

  - **Access Control:**

    A key element of data governance is the establishment of access control policies. These policies dictate who can access certain data and with what privileges. Implementing a strict access control system ensures that only authorized users can view, modify, or use data, reducing the risk of unauthorized access from both inside and outside the organization. This control is often supported by strong authentication mechanisms and audit trails that monitor and record all data-related activity.

  - **Data encryption:**

    Encryption is a well-established practice in data

protection, ensuring that information is protected during transmission and storage. Data governance must include the adoption of advanced encryption techniques to protect data both at rest (data at rest) and in transit (data in transit). This approach is particularly relevant for sensitive and personal data, ensuring that even in the event of a security breach, the data cannot be easily used by malicious actors.

- **Ensure regulatory compliance:**
The regulatory environment in which organizations operate is increasingly complex and constantly evolving. Data governance is critical to ensuring that data and analytics strategies comply with applicable laws and regulations, thus avoiding legal penalties and protecting corporate reputation.
  - **Regulatory monitoring:**
  Data governance includes the responsibility to constantly monitor the regulations that apply to the industry and geography in which the organization operates. This continuous monitoring allows internal data management policies to be adapted so that they are always aligned with legal requirements, such as the

General Data Protection Regulation (GDPR) in Europe or the California Consumer Privacy Act (CCPA) in the United States. This process requires close collaboration between legal, IT, and data governance teams.

- **Data Retention Policy Management:** Establishing data retention and deletion policies is another critical aspect of governance, necessary to ensure compliance with privacy and data protection regulations. These policies must clearly state how long data can be stored and when it must be deleted, based on its nature and legal provisions. Proper data lifecycle management not only ensures compliance, but also helps optimize storage usage and reduce the risk associated with keeping outdated or unnecessary data.

Data Security in BI

Data security is a key pillar in ensuring the reliability of information and ensuring that business decisions are based on solid and healthy data. In the context of Business Intelligence, data protection is not only an operational necessity, but a strategic requirement to protect the company's information assets and support stakeholder trust.

Let's delve into the role that data security plays within the context of Business Intelligence:

- **Ensure the confidentiality of sensitive data:**
  In the BI domain, data privacy is paramount, especially when handling sensitive information such as personal, financial, or proprietary data. Protecting such information is essential not only to comply with current regulations, such as the GDPR, but also to maintain the company's reputation and prevent potential economic or legal damage.

  This implies:

  - **Authorized Access:**
    Access to data must be strictly controlled to prevent unauthorized access, which could compromise the confidentiality of the information. Implementing access control mechanisms, such as multi-factor authentication (MFA), ensures that only users with the necessary permissions can access critical data. In addition, adopting identity and access management (IAM) policies allows you to monitor and regulate access based on user

roles and responsibilities, reducing the risk of inappropriate or fraudulent access.

- **Data encryption:**
  Encryption plays a crucial role in protecting data, both during transmission and storage. The use of advanced cryptographic algorithms ensures that data remains inaccessible to unauthorized third parties, even in the event of interception or theft. In a BI environment, where data is constantly being processed and transmitted, end-to-end encryption, along with secure cryptographic key management, is an essential defense against cyber threats.

- **Protect data from cyberattacks:**
  Business Intelligence platforms, with their ability to aggregate and analyze vast volumes of corporate data, are a primary target for cyberattacks. Data security in this context therefore becomes a priority to prevent breaches that could lead to financial loss, reputational damage or legal penalties.
  This involves:

- **Continuous monitoring:**
  Continuous monitoring is crucial to detect any suspicious activity early. The integration of Intrusion

Detection System (IDS) and Intrusion Prevention System (IPS) systems allows you to quickly identify and respond to unauthorized access attempts or anomalies in user behavior. Additionally, artificial intelligence (AI)-based behavioral analytics can improve detection capability by identifying evolving attack patterns that may be missed by traditional security systems.

- **Regular security updates:**
  The constant evolution of cyber threats requires that security systems be kept up to date.
  This includes not only applying security patches and updating firewalls and antiviruses, but also continuously reviewing security policies and network protocols.
  In a BI environment, where applications can interact with a wide range of data sources, maintaining a high standard of security requires a proactive and coordinated approach.

- **Prevent data loss:**
  Data protection is not limited to preventing unauthorized access or cyberattacks, but also includes the prevention of data loss, whether due

to human error or technical failures. Ensuring business continuity and information availability is crucial to the success of BI operations.
To achieve this:

- **Backup and Recovery:**
  Regular backup processes are essential for data security, ensuring that information can be restored in the event of loss or corruption. Backup strategies should include multiple copies of data, stored in different locations, and periodic verification of their integrity. In addition, a well-defined disaster recovery plan must be in place to ensure a rapid return to operational normality in the event of adverse events, minimizing downtime and impact on business operations.

- **Staff training:**
  Continuous staff training is a key element in preventing data loss. Even the best technology solutions can be ineffective if not supported by users who are aware of threats and good security practices. In a BI context, where data is constantly manipulated and shared, raising employee awareness of security risks and the procedures to be followed to mitigate those risks

is crucial. This includes education on how to recognize phishing attempts, the importance of secure password management, and adopting prudent behavior when handling sensitive information.

Successful Use Case

In this chapter, we'll explore different stories to understand how companies like yours have harnessed the full potential of data to achieve significant milestones.

Through these tangible examples, we will see how D&A and BI translate into tangible results and improve business decisions.

Companies that have benefited from D&A and BI

Analyzing the success stories of companies that have successfully implemented D&A and BI reveals a compelling picture of the opportunities and transformations that these technologies can bring to the corporate world. Examining such cases not only provides inspiration but also offers valuable lessons on how to overcome industry challenges and improve overall performance.

Walmart's experience demonstrates how strategic, technologically advanced data management can completely transform an organization, making it more efficient, responsive, and competitive. The combination of predictive analytics, supply chain optimization and AI and ML integration has become a model of excellence for all companies looking to gain an edge in the global marketplace.

Walmart has invested in data management systems that use the latest big data technologies and machine learning algorithms to analyze massive volumes of historical information from sales and workflows. Through this analysis, the company is able to accurately anticipate demand trends for each product. This predictive ability allows Walmart to:

- **Optimize inventory**:
  Reducing overstocking while ensuring that the products consumers demand are always available on the shelves. This is especially important in a context where consumer preferences can vary by season, region, and even weather events.

- **Reduce operating costs**:
  Optimizing inventory levels allows Walmart to minimize inventory management costs, including storage fees and losses due to unsold products. Thanks to the accuracy offered by predictive models, the company can also reduce the risk of *stock-outs*, which is one of the leading causes of lost sales in the retail sector.

- **Optimize logistics and distribution**:
  Walmart uses a *just-in-time logistics* system that relies on constant monitoring of demand across different stores. This allows deliveries to be scheduled dynamically, improving distribution

efficiency and reducing warehouse downtime.

Walmart's data-driven approach is not limited to operational optimization, but extends to Business Intelligence: through interactive dashboards and advanced reporting systems, managers can monitor company performance in real time, evaluating metrics such as sales, stocks and profits.

This level of visibility and control enables fast, data-driven decision-making, reinforcing the effectiveness of business strategies.

Walmart has not stopped at adopting existing technologies but is committed to continuous innovation, exploring new solutions based on Artificial Intelligence and the Internet of Things (IoT): the company has begun experimenting with robotics for warehouse automation and real-time analytics to further improve the efficiency of its operations.

Mastercard continues to expand its fraud prevention capabilities, integrating emerging technologies such as advanced artificial intelligence, deep learning, and real-time predictive analytics.

The approach taken demonstrates how the strategic use of D&A, combined with artificial intelligence, can not only improve the security of the payments industry, but also offer a sustainable competitive advantage.

Customer trust, transaction security, and optimization of company resources all become interconnected elements that strengthen the company's leadership position.

Mastercard has developed a sophisticated real-time transaction monitoring infrastructure that leverages Big Data and Artificial Intelligence technologies to identify suspicious behavior. Every day, millions of transactions are examined and analyzed by algorithms designed to detect anomalous patterns, based on a vast amount of historical and contextual data.

Among the parameters monitored are:

- **Expense models**:
  The algorithms look at users' spending habits, such as transaction frequency, amount, and locations, to detect anomalies that could indicate a fraud attempt.

- **Geolocation**:
  Advanced geolocation systems help detect suspicious transactions, such as when a purchase is made in a location a few minutes away from another transaction.

- **Card behavior**:
  Cards can be monitored to assess behavior against spending limits and typical transactions, allowing you to detect unusual usage that could indicate fraud.

The integration of machine learning algorithms allows Mastercard to continuously improve its ability to predict and detect fraud.

Algorithms are constantly "trained" with new data, refining predictive models that can identify new threats before they materialize.

ML allows you to:

- Adapt in real time to new types of emerging fraud, improving the effectiveness of the system in preventing attacks that have not yet been cataloged.

- Detect anomalies with increasing accuracy, reducing false positives (legitimate transactions that were incorrectly blocked) and increasing the success rate in blocking fraudulent ones.

Amazon is a case in point of how D&A and BI can be integrated to optimize logistics operations on a global scale. The effective use of D&A and BI has allowed Amazon to build a highly scalable and flexible logistics system, which represents a significant competitive advantage. Continuous innovations, such as the development of drone delivery and the implementation of artificial intelligence to further improve efficiency, ensure that Amazon remains a leader in the e-commerce industry.

One of the most innovative aspects of Amazon's approach is the use of D&A for predictive demand analysis.

The company collects and analyzes huge amounts of data from different sources:

- **Purchase transactions**:

  By tracking purchases in real-time and analyzing sales history, Amazon is able to predict future customer needs with extreme accuracy.

- **Shipping and logistics**:

  Shipment data, such as delivery times, transport routes and volumes handled, are continuously analyzed to optimize routes and transit times, reducing logistics costs.

- **Customer feedback**:
  Feedback and review analysis provides actionable insights to improve service by quickly identifying any issues related to product availability or delivery.

The integration of these sources allows Amazon to deploy machine learning models to predict future demand with astonishing accuracy.

This allows the company to maintain optimal inventory levels, avoiding both overstocking, which could result in high storage costs, and lack of availability, which could reduce customer satisfaction.

Amazon's logistics infrastructure is designed to minimize delivery times, a key factor in maintaining high standards of customer service. With advanced data analytics and BI, Amazon can make fast, informed decisions that continuously improve its operational efficiency. Real-time monitoring of each step of the delivery process allows you to:

- **Optimize shipping routes**:
  based on geospatial and traffic data, reducing transit times.

- **Dynamically adapt resources**:
  based on market conditions, such as seasonal
  fluctuations or spikes in demand, such as during the
  holiday season or *Prime Day*.

NETFLIX

Netflix has been able to transform the entertainment industry by using D&A and AI as fundamental tools for personalizing the user experience.

Using an advanced machine learning architecture, the company analyzes massive amounts of data related to viewing habits, gender preferences, and user feedback. This ability to process information at scale has allowed Netflix to develop a system of personalized recommendations, one of the distinctive features of the platform.

Netflix collects detailed data about user behavior, including:

- **Viewing time**:

  Every viewing session is tracked, including the exact moment a user pauses or stops a show.

- **Genre preferences**:

  Based on the content displayed, the system recognizes personal tastes and suggests related programs.

- **Explicit feedback**:

  User ratings and reviews are used to improve future recommendations.

- **Aggregate behaviors**:

  By analyzing the habits of millions of users, Netflix can identify patterns of behavior on a global scale or in certain geographic regions.

This data is used to train machine learning models that predict what content a user is most inclined to watch. This approach has proven crucial in increasing engagement and reducing churn rate. In fact, by providing tailored recommendations, Netflix reduces the time a user spends searching for content and extends their stay on the platform.

Netflix uses advanced predictive modeling tools to analyze which genres, themes, or storytelling styles are most in demand in a given time period or region. This strategy has optimized investments, ensuring that resources are allocated to projects with the highest return potential, both in terms of views and subscriptions. In addition, real-time performance monitoring allows you to quickly adjust your marketing strategy, improving the visibility of less popular content.

AIR LINES

Delta Airlines has taken an innovative and pioneering approach to using D&A and BI to improve aircraft maintenance, which is crucial to ensuring both safety and operational efficiency. This strategy is part of a broader context of digital transformation that is redefining the practices of the aviation industry, with an increasing emphasis on the intelligent use of data to optimize internal processes and improve the reliability of operations.

A central element of this transformation is the integration of IoT (**I**nternet **of T**hings) sensors on board aircraft. These sensors, distributed across several critical components, collect real-time operational data on a wide range of key parameters, including engine condition, navigation systems, hydraulics, and control systems. Data is constantly transmitted to a centralized platform, where it is processed through advanced BI models. These models, based on machine learning and artificial intelligence algorithms, analyze the information to provide a detailed, updated and dynamic view of the operating conditions of each aircraft.

This approach has enabled Delta Airlines to adopt predictive maintenance, a paradigm that revolutionizes traditional scheduled or reactive maintenance models.

In a traditional model, maintenance takes place on a time-based basis or following a failure, while predictive maintenance allows preventive intervention by identifying components or systems that may show signs of wear or future malfunctions.

Predictive algorithms use *pattern recognition* techniques to identify anomalies or degradation trends, allowing maintenance interventions to be planned with greater precision and timeliness.

A significant impact of this strategy is the reduction of aircraft downtime, which is a major source of operational and cost inefficiencies in the aviation industry. By reducing unexpected breakdowns and minimizing unplanned disruptions, Delta can improve fleet availability, increasing flight on-time and customer satisfaction. In an industry where operating margins are often very tight, optimizing fleet management results in a significant competitive advantage.

The use of data is not limited to aircraft maintenance alone, but is integrated into a broader digital ecosystem that spans multiple aspects of Delta Airlines' operations.

E.g.: *The data collected by the sensors can be used to optimize flight performance, improve fuel efficiency and reduce environmental impact, issues that are becoming increasingly relevant in the context of a growing focus on sustainability in the air transport sector.*

Positive impacts and results achieved

The integration of Data & Analytics (D&A) and Business Intelligence (BI) technologies into the business context has proven to have a transformative impact, significantly improving the quality of decisions and optimizing overall results.

Exploring the positive effects of these technologies in detail, it emerges that they can revolutionize customer understanding, optimize business operations and mitigate risks, leading to more informed and proactive management.

Improve customer understanding:
One of the most important contributions that D&A and BI offer to companies is the ability to deepen the knowledge of their customers. Businesses can leverage these tools to collect and analyze a wide range of data from different sources, such as online interactions, shopping behaviors,

personal preferences, and post-purchase feedback. This detailed analysis allows you to build complete and accurate customer profiles, facilitating market segmentation and personalization of offers.

For example, an e-commerce company can use D&A to examine users' browsing data, identifying patterns of behavior that suggest specific interests or emerging needs. Through machine learning algorithms, it is possible to predict future purchasing behaviors, allowing the company to offer personalized recommendations and targeted promotions. This level of in-depth understanding not only increases the likelihood of conversion, but also strengthens customer loyalty, improving the overall experience and increasing customer lifetime value.

Optimize operations:

D&A and BI are essential tools for optimizing business operations, allowing companies to analyze their activities in real time and identify inefficiencies or areas for improvement. The ability to monitor and analyze operational data allows you to make faster, more informed decisions based on hard evidence rather than past insights or experience.

A concrete example of this application can be seen in manufacturing companies that use D&A to monitor the entire production process. Through IoT sensors and BI systems, the data collected along the production line is analyzed to identify bottlenecks, waste of resources or variations in machine performance. This analysis allows you to optimize your workflow, ensuring that resources are allocated efficiently and that operations are conducted with maximum productivity. By reducing waste and improving operational efficiency, companies can achieve significant cost savings and increase their competitiveness in the market.

Prevent risks:

The ability to prevent and mitigate risks is another crucial benefit offered by D&A and BI. These technologies allow companies to anticipate potential problems, acting in a preventive rather than reactive manner. Through data analysis, anomalies or suspicious patterns can be detected early on that could indicate imminent risks, such as fraud, quality issues, or operational failures.

In the financial sector, for example, advanced data analytics allows transactions to be monitored in real time to identify anomalous behavior that could indicate fraud. With predictive models and machine learning, businesses can identify suspicious patterns and take immediate action, blocking transactions and minimizing losses. Similarly, in the manufacturing sector, the analysis of data from production lines can reveal variations in process parameters that suggest possible quality defects. By intervening early, the company can prevent the production of defective batches, thereby reducing recall costs and improving customer satisfaction.

The implementation of D&A and BI goes beyond the simple adoption of advanced technologies; it requires the development of a strongly data-oriented corporate culture. The companies that can take full advantage of these technologies are those that integrate data analysis into the daily decision-making process, transforming data into a fundamental strategic asset. This integration allows companies to react more quickly to market changes, innovate more effectively and build a sustainable competitive advantage over time.

AI/ML integration use case

The integration of Artificial Intelligence and Machine Learning into Business Intelligence platforms has led to a radical transformation in the way companies can analyze data and make informed decisions.
These advanced technologies not only automate and accelerate analytics processes, but also enable deeper

insights and more accurate predictions, thereby improving the competitiveness and operational efficiency of companies.

Let's look at some concrete cases of AI and ML integration:

Salesforce, one of the most advanced and widespread Customer Relationship Management (CRM) platforms globally, has been able to evolve and adapt to the needs of the contemporary market by integrating Predictive Analysis features that greatly enhance the BI capabilities made available to its users.

This innovation is part of a broader context of digital transformation that sees the use of Machine Learning (ML) and AI algorithms as key tools to improve data management and support strategic decisions increasingly based on quantitative evidence.

The introduction of predictive models within the platform

allows companies to analyze historical and current sales data with extreme precision, highlighting patterns and trends that could remain hidden using traditional methods of analysis.

This allows not only to obtain a clearer view of past performance, but above all to outline future scenarios, supporting sales teams in making informed and proactive decisions.

With these models, Salesforce offers the ability to accurately predict the evolution of customer behavior, identifying potential opportunities for upselling and cross-selling. In this way, sales teams can implement customized strategies that can maximize revenue and improve operational efficiency.

One of the most relevant applications of predictive analytics concerns the management of sales opportunities. The ML algorithms used by Salesforce analyze a vast amount of data from previous interactions, buying behaviors, customer feedback, and sales cycles. This data is processed to generate accurate predictions about the likelihood of a successful sale, allowing sales managers to allocate resources more efficiently and focus on opportunities that are more likely to convert. The early identification of emerging trends allows companies to anticipate customer needs, responding promptly to new requests or adapting the offer in real time.

Another crucial aspect enhanced by predictive analytics concerns the definition of pricing strategies: through the analysis of data relating to customer response to different price ranges and promotions, companies can adopt dynamic pricing policies, capable of quickly adapting to fluctuations in market demand. This approach allows you to not only maximize revenues during periods of high demand, but also to manage any reductions more effectively in sales volumes, thus improving overall profitability.

A further benefit of integrating predictive analytics is the ability to create highly detailed and personalized customer profiles: thanks to the combination of behavioral data, expressed preferences and purchase histories, Salesforce allows companies to develop an accurate picture of their customers, making it easier to offer tailored experiences. Personalization is in fact one of the determining factors in building solid and lasting relationships with customers, as it increases not only satisfaction but also loyalty.

E.g.: Companies can send targeted offers based on specific interests, suggest complementary products to those already purchased, or anticipate customer needs before they are explicitly communicated.

Google Analytics, one of the most advanced and popular web analytics tools globally, has evolved with the integration of AI and machine learning to enhance the analysis of online user behavior. This evolution reflects the growing need for companies to adopt technologies that go beyond simply measuring static data, offering predictive and prescriptive tools that facilitate evidence-based strategic decisions and advanced interaction models.

This integration allows you to identify complex patterns of user behavior that, in a traditional perspective, would be difficult to detect or could be completely overlooked. Thanks to AI, Google Analytics can analyze huge volumes of data related to website interactions, identifying correlations between seemingly unrelated variables, such as browsing patterns, bounce rate, time spent on certain pages, and conversion paths. This capability allows website operators to gain a deeper understanding of which pages or elements have the greatest impact on the user experience and how this affects the overall navigation path.

One of the most innovative aspects of AI in Google Analytics is its ability to go beyond simply describing users' past behavior, suggesting concrete and targeted actions to improve site performance and user experience. For example, through the analysis of historical and real-time data, the algorithm can suggest structural changes to the design of the site, such as optimizing the arrangement of content or changing navigation flows to reduce the abandonment rate (*bounce rate*) and increase the dwell time. AI can also identify which sections of the site tend to generate obstacles for users, allowing specific interventions to be implemented to make navigation smoother and more intuitive, improving general usability.

Another area where Google Analytics AI offers significant added value is the personalization of digital marketing campaigns: AI-driven analytics allow you to segment your audience more effectively, based not only on demographics or geographic data, but also on explicit and implicit behaviors and preferences detected through interactions on the site.
This allows you to create highly targeted and relevant marketing campaigns, tailoring specific messages and

offers to each segment.

AI-driven analysis also makes it possible to implement a logic of continuous optimization, in which the constant monitoring of user behavior feeds a virtuous cycle of improvement.

Through this process, you can identify actions that lead to increased user engagement and, as a result, better results in terms of conversions and returns on investment (ROI).

This ability to adapt and optimize in real time gives companies a significant competitive advantage, allowing them to respond quickly to consumer needs and constantly changing market dynamics.

IBM Watson Analytics has introduced advanced predictive analytics capabilities specifically designed for the HR industry, giving organizations powerful tools for managing people. By analyzing historical and present employee data, IBM Watson can predict staff turnover, identify factors that influence employee satisfaction and suggest actions to improve operational efficiency and retention.

With predictive models, companies can identify employees at risk of leaving the company in advance and implement targeted strategies to retain talent, such as personalized professional development programs or improvements in working conditions. In addition, analyzing data on employee performance and well-being allows you to identify areas for improvement in human resource management, helping to create a more productive and rewarding work environment.

IBM Watson Analytics not only provides predictions, but

also allows you to explore different "*what-if*" scenarios, helping HR leaders make strategic decisions based on accurate simulations. This approach allows companies to better align their human resources with the organization's strategic goals, improving productivity and reducing costs associated with turnover and poor performance.

These use cases demonstrate how the integration of AI and ML with Business Intelligence not only enhances the analytical capabilities of companies, but fundamentally transforms the way data is used to make strategic decisions. Companies that adopt these advanced technologies can gain a significant competitive advantage, thanks to deeper insights, more accurate predictions, and highly optimized operational strategies.

Combining BI and AI technologies

The integration between Business Intelligence and advanced Artificial Intelligence technologies represents a crucial evolutionary step for modern companies, revolutionizing the way data is analyzed and used to support decision-making.

This combination not only optimizes existing business operations, but also introduces new potential, making organizations more competitive and able to adapt quickly to an ever-changing market.

- **Automating analytics with AI/ML:**
  One of the most obvious benefits of merging BI and AI/ML is the automation of data analytics. Traditionally, the data analysis process requires a significant investment of time and resources, often spent on repetitive tasks such as data collection, cleaning, and preparation. With the introduction of machine learning (ML) algorithms, these processes can be automated, freeing analysts from the need to perform manual tasks and allowing them to focus on more strategic tasks.

- **Deeper and more accurate insights:**
  The integration of AI and ML into BI platforms

overcomes the limitations of traditional analytics, offering a data exploration capability that goes beyond descriptive and retrospective analysis. AI techniques, particularly those based on neural networks and deep learning, are capable of process large volumes of unstructured data, identifying hidden correlations and predicting future trends with a much higher degree of accuracy than conventional methods.

- **Responsiveness and business agility:**
  The adoption of AI and ML within BI platforms not only improves the quality of insights, but makes companies more responsive and agile in responding to market dynamics. The ability to analyze data in real-time is particularly beneficial in highly variable industries, such as e-commerce or retail, where market conditions can change rapidly and require an immediate response.

The integration of BI with AI and ML is therefore not limited to improving existing processes, but also allows you to explore new business models and operational strategies that can confer a sustainable competitive advantage. However, to take full advantage of these technologies, it is essential for companies to invest not only in technological infrastructure, but also in the development of specific skills. Continuous training and upskilling of staff is crucial to ensure that the organization is able to effectively manage digital transformation and adapt to the new challenges and opportunities presented by the fusion of BI and AI.

The Continuous Evolution of D&A and BI

The dynamic world of Data & Analytics and Business Intelligence is in a state of constant transformation, driven by both technological innovations and the growing demands of the corporate world.

The evolution of these disciplines not only redefines the way organizations collect and analyze data, but also profoundly influences business strategies, improving the ability of enterprises to make informed and timely decisions.

Let's explore how the latest trends are redefining the way companies conceive and leverage data analytics:

- **Emerging technologies:**
  The emergence of advanced technologies such as Artificial Intelligence, Machine Learning and predictive analytics represents a turning point in the

data analytics landscape. These technologies are transforming BI from a retrospective reporting tool to a predictive and prescriptive engine capable of anticipating business needs and proactively responding to market changes. The integration of AI into BI platforms allows it to go beyond the analysis of historical data, allowing for more accurate predictions and complex pattern identifications that would otherwise go unnoticed.

Machine Learning stands out for its ability to learn from data and improve its performance over time without the need for explicit programming. This allows us to develop increasingly precise and adaptive analysis models, capable of recognizing and responding to new trends and anomalies as they arise. For example, the implementation of deep learning algorithms in BI analytics allows for the processing of massive volumes of unstructured data, such as images and text, offering insights that were previously out of reach.

- **Cloud-based models:**
  The adoption of cloud infrastructure represents another significant shift in the way companies manage D&A and BI. Cloud solutions provide flexible

and scalable access to compute and storage resources, reducing the need for upfront investments in expensive and complex hardware. This model allows companies to quickly scale their operations in response to growing demands, without compromising performance or security.

The integration of BI platforms with the cloud also fosters greater collaboration and data sharing across business departments, fostering a data-driven decision-making culture. In addition, cloud solutions facilitate the implementation of advanced analytics models, such as predictive analytics and machine learning, without requiring dedicated on-premises infrastructure. This allows companies to access high-level analysis tools at a low cost and to take advantage of the latest technological innovations with greater ease.

- **Access to real-time data:**
The ability to access real-time data has become a strategic necessity for modern enterprises, which must respond quickly to market changes and customer needs. BI infrastructure is evolving to support the management and analysis of continuous data flows, improving the timeliness and accuracy of

business decisions.

Instant access to up-to-date information allows businesses to monitor operations in real-time, identifying issues or opportunities as they arise. For example, in the retail industry, real-time analysis of sales and customer behaviors can drive decisions about pricing, promotions, and inventory management, improving operational efficiency and increasing revenue. In addition, the ability to process data in real time allows you to optimize the customer experience, offering quick and personalized responses to customer needs.

The continuous evolution of D&A and BI is not only a response to technological advancement, but also offers a unique opportunity for companies to remain competitive in a rapidly changing market. Investing in emerging technologies, adopting cloud-based models, and leveraging access to real-time data are key strategies for maintaining a competitive edge.

However, to take full advantage of these innovations, it is essential for companies to develop a data-driven culture, where advanced analytics becomes an integral part of daily decision-making. The ability to constantly adapt and innovate will be key to fully exploiting the potential offered by the evolution of D&A and BI.

Ethics in the use of data and Bias in analysis

Ethics is one of the fundamental principles in D&A and BI, influencing crucial aspects such as public trust, the integrity of analytics, and the impact of business decisions.

Integrating robust ethical practices ensures that data usage is transparent, accountable, and compliant with regulatory and societal expectations.

Ethics in data analytics and BI solutions

Ethics plays a crucial role in the entire lifecycle of data and analytics, directly influencing the public's perception of the company and the quality of business decisions.

Let's look in more detail at some key aspects that highlight the importance of ethics in this context:

- **Public Trust:**
  An ethical approach to data analytics is essential for building and maintaining public trust. Transparency and ethical responsibility are the pillars on which this trust is based.

  Key elements include:

    - **Open communication:**
      Transparency requires open communication about how data is collected, managed, and used. This clarity builds public trust in the company's practices.

    - **Respect for privacy:**
      Demonstrating an ethical commitment means respecting data privacy. The

company must ensure that personal
information is treated with the strictest
confidentiality and according to
applicable laws.

- **Analysis integrity:**
Ethics ensures the integrity of analyses, ensuring
that data is treated impartially and accurately.
Key points include:

  - **Avoid manipulation:**
  Ethics dictate that you avoid biasing or
  manipulating data to influence results. The
  analysis must faithfully reflect reality and not
  be distorted for specific purposes.

  - **Fair access to data:**
  All actors involved must have equal access to
  data. Ethics requires avoiding excessive
  privileges to certain groups, ensuring a fair
  basis for analysis.

- **Informed business decisions:**
Ethics in the data analysis process is crucial to
ensure that business decisions are based on truthful
information and respect ethical values.
Key elements are:

Social Impact:

>   Considering the social impact of business decisions is an integral part of ethics. Companies need to assess how their actions will affect society.

- **Sustainability:**

>   Ethics requires considering environmental impact and sustainability in business decisions.
>
>   The analysis must consider ecological and social aspects in order to promote responsible decisions.

Ethical responsibility of companies

Companies have a fundamental responsibility to adopt ethical practices in data analysis, considering the impacts of their decisions on people, society and the environment. This implies:

- **Awareness of the implications:**

  - **Sensitive data:**

>   Companies must be especially careful when handling sensitive or potentially invasive data, such as personal or financial information. Awareness of the ethical implications of such

data requires a careful assessment of the impacts that could result from their manipulation.

- **Transparency:**
  Understanding the ethical implications also involves transparent communication with stakeholders. Companies must be able to clearly explain how data is used, providing detailed information on the collection, analysis and storage processes.

Ethical governance:

- **Business Decision Guidance:**
  Implementing ethical governance means providing clear guidance for business decisions related to data. This governance must reflect core ethical values and establish guidelines to ensure the ethical use of data at all stages of its lifecycle.

- **Stakeholder involvement:** Ethical governance should involve stakeholders, including employees, customers, and other key actors. Consulting with these stakeholders in ethical policymaking helps to ensure that the guidelines are representative of the needs and concerns of all actors involved.

Transparency and Accountability

These principles are essential for building stakeholder trust and ensuring a responsible approach to data analysis.

Let's take a closer look at these key elements:

- **Clear communication:**

  - **Decision Making:**
    Transparency requires clear communication about decision-making processes. Companies need to make explicit how data is collected, analyzed, and used. A transparent presentation of these processes contributes to a comprehensive understanding of stakeholders.

  Access and purpose:
  Transparency extends to access to data and why it's used. Companies should clearly inform who has access to data and for what purpose. Not only does this promote trust, but it also helps to avoid misunderstandings or concerns on the part of users.

- **Responding to consequences:**

Assumption of responsibility:
> Accountability implies that companies are prepared to take responsibility for the consequences of their actions. In the event of errors or ethical violations, it is essential for companies to immediately acknowledge what happened, apologize if necessary, and take corrective action.

- **Search and remediation processes:**
> When problems occur, accountability requires companies to initiate research processes to understand the root causes. Additionally, they should implement corrective measures to prevent the same mistakes from happening again in the future.

Relevance of Bias in D&A models and analyses

Bias in models and analyses is one of the most relevant and complex issues in the field of Data & Analytics, as it can compromise the validity, reliability and objectivity of the results obtained. This phenomenon can have significant consequences on business decision-making, generating misinterpretations of data and leading to strategic choices based on biased information. The presence of bias reduces the ability of analyses to faithfully represent reality, risking perpetuating inequalities or distorting predictions. To ensure an unbiased and fact-based assessment, it is crucial to understand the different forms of *bias* and take steps to mitigate their impact.

- **Bias:**

  - **Selection Bias:**

    It occurs when the data sample used for the analysis is not representative of the entire population or phenomenon studied.

    This type of bias can result from inadequate data choice, which excludes, for example, significant segments of the population or ignores relevant factors.

    One of the most serious consequences of this type of bias is the distortion of conclusions since the analysis will not be adequately calibrated with respect to the diversity of the context.

  - **Temporal bias:**

    It occurs when the analysis is based on data

limited to a specific period of time, without taking into account subsequent dynamics and evolutions.

This type of bias can be particularly problematic in rapidly changing industries, such as technology or finance. For example, the use of data collected before an economic crisis could lead to forecasts that are no longer valid in the post-crisis context. Failure to include more up-to-date data or underestimating structural changes can lead to outdated decisions or decisions that are not relevant to current dynamics, thus compromising the company's ability to adapt to new market conditions.

- **Confirmation Bias:**

  It is one of the most insidious cognitive distortions since it involves the very interpretative process of data analysis. It occurs when the analyst, consciously or unconsciously, seeks confirmation of pre-existing preconceptions or hypotheses, ignoring or minimizing data that could contradict those beliefs. This type of bias can lead to selective use of information and conclusions that only reinforce existing thought patterns, reducing the ability to explore new perspectives or consider alternative solutions.

- **Bias in training data:**

  In machine learning models, bias in training data is a critical issue.

  ML models learn from the examples provided during the training phase, so any bias in the data will be assimilated by the model and replicated in its predictions.

- **Mitigation strategies:**

- **Data Auditing:**

  Regular data auditing is one of the most effective practices for identifying and mitigating *biases* within datasets used for analysis. This process consists of a systematic and critical review of the data, with a focus on their representativeness, completeness and balance.

  Auditing must assess whether all relevant population groups or significant variables have been adequately included in the sample, avoiding underrepresentations that could distort the results.

Effective data auditing not only aims to identify the presence of bias, but must also propose solutions to correct it, such as collecting additional data to balance the sample or adopting statistical techniques to neutralize the influence of potentially problematic variables. Auditing should be an ongoing process, as data and contexts change over time; Maintaining a regular review allows analytical models to be adapted to new realities, ensuring the relevance and reliability of the analyses in the long term.

- **Team diversification:**

  Another key strategy for mitigating *bias* is diversifying analytics teams. *Biases* often stem from implicit or unconscious biases, which can be difficult to recognize within homogeneous groups. Therefore, the diversification of staff, in terms of cultural background, personal experiences, professional skills and ideological perspectives, can play a crucial role in the recognition and management of *bias*. Teams made up of individuals with diverse backgrounds are more likely to identify potential biases that might otherwise go unnoticed, thanks to increased sensitivity and collective awareness.

The presence of different perspectives in decision-making and analytical processes leads to a more critical evaluation of the models and data used, thus increasing the possibility of discovering and correcting any biases. Fostering an inclusive culture is not only a matter of social equity, but also of improving the quality of analytics and the ability to respond more appropriately to different market and customer needs.

- **Strengthening ethics in analysis:**
Implementing ethical practices is an essential component of addressing bias in data and analytical models. Fostering a corporate culture that emphasizes the importance of ethics means encouraging awareness of bias and promoting a transparent approach to data management and analysis interpretation.

Bias awareness cannot be seen as just a technical problem, but must be integrated into the broader framework of business ethics and social responsibility.

An ethical approach to analytics requires data professionals to be constantly vigilant in recognizing the limitations and potential biases inherent in their models.

This implies the need to openly communicate the risks related to bias, both internally and externally to the organization, making transparent the methods used to mitigate these risks.

In this context, transparency is not limited to the disclosure of results, but must also extend to the explanation of methodological choices, algorithms used and data sources used, to ensure that all stakeholders can understand and assess the integrity of the analytical process.

The adoption of specific codes of ethics for data analytics professionals can further strengthen the commitment to responsible and impartial analytical practice. Such codes should include clear guidelines on how to address *bias*, promoting the adoption of auditing strategies, team diversification, and ongoing training on the ethical risks associated with data use.

Role of Ethical Regulations and Guidelines

Regulations and ethical guidelines are a key pillar for providing clear directions and establishing shared standards within the complex D&A and BI landscape.

These regulations are vital to ensure that business practices are not only efficient but also ethical, meeting globally accepted standards:

- **GDPR and Personal Data Protection:**

  The European Union's **G**eneral **D**ata **P**rotection **R**egulation (**GDPR**) is a cornerstone in protecting the privacy and security of personal data.

  This regulation requires companies to take strict measures to ensure data security and privacy. Among the key aspects, there is the obligation to acquire explicit consent for the collection and processing of personal data, ensuring that individuals have control over their information.

- **Sectoral rules:**

  In many industries, there are specific rules governing the use of data and analytics, tailored to the needs and specificities of each sector. In the U.S. healthcare industry, the **H**ealth **I**nsurance **P**ortability and **A**ccountability **A**ct (**HIPAA**) sets strict standards for protecting health data. These policies are designed to ensure that sensitive patient information is treated with the utmost confidentiality and security.

- **International Ethical Guidelines:**
  International ethical guidelines play a key role in guiding ethical behavior in the implementation of D&A and BI technologies.

  IEEE (**I**nstitute of **E**lectrical and **E**lectronics **E**ngineers) and the European Union's AI Ethics Guidelines provide guiding principles for the development and ethical implementation of artificial intelligence technologies. These guidelines emphasize the importance of accountability, transparency and respect for human rights in the use of advanced technologies.

Key Concepts

- **Data Analysis Algorithms:**

  Sequential routing of instructions used to perform operations on data, including those used for statistical and predictive analysis.

- **Real-Time Data Analysis:**

  Process of examining and interpreting data as soon as it is generated, allowing for immediate response to changing conditions.

- **Risk Analysis:**
  The process of identifying, assessing, and managing business risks that may affect the achievement of objectives.

- **Sentiment Analysis:**
  The process of determining the opinion or tone of a text, often applied to customer interactions to gauge satisfaction or perception of a brand or product.

- **Online Analytical Processing (OLAP) Analysis:**
  A data analysis technique that allows you to explore data from different perspectives, providing a more complete view of your business.

- **Predictive analytics:**
  Using statistical models and algorithms to predict future outcomes based on historical data.

- **Big Data:**
  A term that refers to datasets that are huge and complex in size, often beyond the capabilities of

traditional data management tools.

- **Business Intelligence (BI):**
  Discipline that deals with the transformation of data into useful information for decision-making.

- **Churn Rate:**
  This is the percentage of customers who abandon a service or terminate a subscription in a defined period of time. It measures customer retention, with a high value indicating rapid loss and a low value reflecting high retention.

- **Cloud Computing:**
  Provision of computing services, such as servers, storage, databases, networking, via the internet.

- **Dashboard:**
  Graphical interface that allows you to visualize data in a concise and intuitive way.

- **Smart Dashboard:**
  A dashboard that uses artificial intelligence to dynamically adapt to the user's needs, providing

relevant information in real-time.

- **Data & Analytics (D&A):**
  A discipline that deals with the collection, processing, and interpretation of data to extract useful information.

- **Unstructured data:**
  Information that doesn't follow a predefined schema or format, such as free text, images, or videos.

- **Data scientist:**
  A highly skilled professional who combines multidisciplinary skills to transform raw data into meaningful insights.

- **Data Visualization:**
  The process of representing data in a clear and intuitive way, using graphs, diagrams, and other tools.

- **Discovery-driven analytics:**
  An analytical approach that allows users to explore data without the need to ask specific questions in

advance.

- **Performance Management:**
  Organizational approach that integrates planning and monitoring processes to ensure that goals are achieved efficiently and effectively.

- **Artificial Intelligence (AI):**
  A discipline that deals with creating systems that can perform tasks that require human intelligence.

- **Decision intelligence:**
  A data-driven decision-making support process.

- **Machine Learning:**
  A field of artificial intelligence that deals with creating models that can learn from data without being explicitly programmed.

- **Operational Optimization:**
  Process of improving business processes to maximize efficiency and reduce costs.

- **Python and R:**
  Programming languages widely used for data

analysis and the development of statistical models and machine learning.

- **Line users:**
  Frontline employees who use BI tools for everyday decisions.

www.ingramcontent.com/pod-product-compliance
Lightning Source LLC
LaVergne TN
LVHW012335060326
832902LV00012B/1888